RECOGNIZING THE SPIRIT WITHIN US:

The Basic Goodness of Human Nature

by

Warren R. Greatrex

Order this book online at www.trafford.com
or email orders@trafford.com

Most Trafford titles are also available at major online book retailers.

Print information available on the last page.

ISBN: 978-1-4120-2473-0 (sc)

Trafford rev. 03/24/2021

www.trafford.com

North America & international
toll-free: 844-688-6899 (USA & Canada)
fax: 812 355 4082

*To Those Who Recognize
That Love is All —
When It's Enlivened
By The Spirit Within*

Acknowledgements

The "seed" of this book was planted many years ago through an emphatic declaration by my brother, Bill: "Boy! That guy John *sure* has a lot to answer for!" I forget the context but he meant the writer of the "Gospel of St. John". I thank him sincerely for this, and for his willingness, and that of his wife Lois, to give their expert advice whenever needed.

Many people have told me that they felt it was time to demonstrate that "beliefs" based on documents "declared to be sacred" in the fourth century, and thus "fixed" in Creeds, ought to be "set aside" in the light of modern scholarship. This "alternative version of events" surrounding Jesus' life, and following upon his death, is for them.

This is not a "scholarly" book. Rather, it arises out of my conviction that a Spirit of Goodness is basic to human nature and that, for example, the story about "The Fall of Man" in the Book of Genesis showed only what certain religious people believed to be true. Therefore it is definitely an alternative way to look at the Bible. It is my own view and I do not claim to be able to prove it. The Introduction will explain why I wrote it.

I should like to thank those friends who have been willing to read preliminary drafts and to offer comments. One in particular, Betty Bergin, has been kind enough to provide a detailed critique, as well as offering strong encouragement; I am most grateful to her. I am indebted as well to John Linford who gave support by sending me his book on a similar theme. Our children have been very supportive, as well.

I pay tribute to the insights of the learned authors mentioned in the Bibliography, and to those who contributed to the volume edited by John Hick. I have relied frequently upon articles in the Oxford Dictionary of the Christian Church and make grateful acknowledgment to the Yearly Meeting of the Religious Society of Friends (Quakers) in Britain for permission to use an extended quotation, that of the "Foundations of a true social order" in Chapter Ten. I have read daily, for more than twenty years, *The Holy Bible, New International Version* which has led me to many new insights; it is with gratitude that I acknowledge using this version for all biblical quotations.

These words of mine appear through the courtesy and expertise of my niece, Sandee Greatrex and her husband Mark Saunders. They also share my belief that through the recognition of the Good Spirit within us and by aligning our consciences and actions with it, we – and those who follow us – will have the opportunity to live in a society respectful of one another and the environment. Their artistry and skill extend, literally, from cover to cover; I am deeply thankful to both of them.

Finally, I acknowledge the steadfast support of Joan, my wife of over fifty years. While dissenting both from the need for my book and also from much of its contents, she nevertheless has always admitted my right to express my views and has many times given me encouragement to continue. And in no way does she dispute my principal theme, but exemplifies it: that a loving spirit exists within us all.

W.R.G. 2003

Table of Contents

Introduction

My book is for those who are willing to believe that there is real meaning and purpose in each person's life here on earth. Such a belief is essential if one is to experience the joy of being alive, day by day, even when things are not going well.

(Note of concern: as this book claims to be of value to both believer and non-believer, I trust readers considering themselves to be of the latter category will understand my difficulty in avoiding mention of God. May I ask that you kindly substitute any word that conveys your understanding that a Spirit of, or Desire for, Goodness does exist in each person, its origin undeclared)

Today we are all neighbours on this tiny, fragile globe. The basic truth is that we are meant to love God and also to love all other people. These two "commandments" were proclaimed centuries ago by the prophet Jeremiah; Jesus quoted him with approval and made it vivid for us by telling the story of the Good Samaritan; and, indeed, this truth has been evidenced in the lives and writings of many persons known to us today. This is the way forward for all humankind, and we have progressed steadily in both understanding and practice. But there is still a long way to go.

Gradually we are coming to realize that compassion and a spirit of reconciliation towards all others is what God most desires, and therefore that the keeping of the second of those two "commandments" is the only way to fulfil the first. Any claim to be observing properly the first, i.e. by declaring, in words and worship, love for God, without steadily practicing the second, is hollow. And this claim is at its most deadly emptiness when its main motive is based upon the promise of "eternal life in heaven". This is because the church, through too many centuries, has sought to use its power to insist upon its members' acceptance of its own doctrine as the essential key to unlocking this promise.

My book was originally conceived as a way to show that this "power approach" of the church is wrong-headed and should be abandoned. Not merely this, but I attempt to show, through this alternate view of how Jesus revealed God's true nature, that it can be taken up even by those who do not believe in God. But this will come to pass only when those of us who are attempting to believe are willing to accept those who (for whatever reason) do not believe, in the same way that Jesus accepted everyone, and that many others also have done: as part of one family, which is all humankind.

This leads directly to the contents of this book. I believe that most of the Western world has taken the humane teaching and example of Jesus to its heart and is no longer obsessed with the Church's dogmas and its insistence upon the essentiality of both credal belief and participation in the sacraments. Indeed, apart from theologians and those choosing to be bound by their pronouncements, Church members of my own communion (Anglican / Episcopal) are gradually weaning themselves away from such dependency, sometimes by introducing less detailed creeds at services and often by welcoming all "persons in good standing in their own Church" to the eucharist, seeing this invitation as an opportunity to extend Jesus' counsel of acceptance to at least some others; of course those attending who are attached to no church remain technically excluded.

This alternative view is therefore set out as one possible explanation for the way that the Christian Church set off on the wrong road – striving for power right from the beginning, albeit with good intentions – and progressing along it, with its apparent "big break" being in reality its doom. Acceptance by Constantine in the fourth century ensured ecclesiastical power only by engendering the attitude of orthodoxy, the human idea that words could encompass the nature of God, and that certain words actually did. This of course led to the concept of heresy for all whose experience of God and understanding of the purposes of Jesus' ministry differed from those who considered themselves to be "right", i.e. orthodox. Although the path of church development has ensured the preservation of Jesus' words and actions during his earthly ministry, they have been buried among accretions that support church doctrine. In addition, the "meaning of Jesus" has been skewed in such a way that his lifetime encounters with others, teaching and healing them, have been subordinated to his death and "what came after". Such unfortunate skewing now needs to be redressed.

Modern insights have demonstrated to the satisfaction of many of us that our awareness of the goodness of life does not depend upon any promise such as "eternal life". Yet "main-stream religion" has for many centuries claimed that membership in one or another particular institution will achieve this promise if, while here on earth, the members will assent to complicated statements about "the nature of God" and also obey rules of conduct laid down for them. However, young people today and indeed many of their parents have seen through this approach and have rightly rejected it.

I too have come to believe that this rejection is probably correct. No longer need one accept the doctrines conceived by men in their endeavours to urge people into salvation by proclaiming, at first, an imminent ending of the world and, later, "exclusive" truth. Twentieth century scholarship has vindicated those who realize that such an approach is folly.

It is therefore time to seek the meaning of our lives, partly through examining the words and actions of others who have "stood alone" in their own times, but mainly through an awareness that within each one of us resides – and resides permanently – a spirit, an actual part of our being, which enables us not only to "choose what is right" but to be thankful and joyful for that choosing.

Your spirit within has to work against many of your instincts, inherited through evolution, and this is where knowledge of how others have achieved this will help you. The purpose of this book is to highlight the life and ministry of one such man, by sweeping away the myth-beliefs that have surrounded him ever since his death. This man's name was Jesus; a man who trusted the spirit within him and so gave us good reason to trust the spirit within each of us.

Thus, here you will find an attempt to set out an alternative view of the primary purpose of Jesus' life and ministry. It was not to proclaim "eternal life in heaven" to be a person's most important goal, but rather to reveal God's will for all humanity. This is that compassion for others, lived out in each person's individual life, should triumph over the inherited instinct of self-survival, which always has been, and remains, a powerful evolutionary drive.

"Jesus no doubt believed in the resurrection, along with many other things that the Jews of his time believed in;... For Jesus, in his time, resurrection was simply not the issue."[1] Those are the words of a highly-respected Christian scholar.

But Paul would not have agreed: not only do his letters insist that Jesus' resurrection was of primary importance, they also loaded its meaning, when linked to his death, with such metaphor and emotion that later readers felt impelled to accept his view, whence has come so much of the "detail" of the Christian faith as taught by the Church. This book will, it is hoped, restore a much-needed balance to the gospel. Did Jesus *clear the way for "true believers"*, by his death and resurrection, as Paul and the Church teach? Or, alternatively, did Jesus *make the way clear for all humanity*, throughout his life, by his teachings, his healings, and his steadfast obedience to his prayerful perception of God's will, right up to and including his death?

After many years of learning, teaching and preaching the view of the Church in respect to the meaning of Jesus' life, I have finally realized that there is too much clutter in organized religion. This clutter, made up of coagulated creeds and complicated ceremonies, needs to be swept aside, in order that the intended meaning of Jesus' life and ministry may be illumined today as clearly as it was to those among whom he moved, almost two thousand years ago. This meaning has become so encrusted with dogma, so hedged about with ritual, that many have despaired of finding it written in the Bible or apparent in the Church's life. Yet it is there, hidden within the clutter, and with patience and common sense, it can be found.

More important still, as you begin to seek it, you will find this intended meaning within yourself as well. It will arise not only from your learning about it, but at the same time it will "light up your life" from within, as you come to realize that you are indeed "on the right track."

This book first offers (in Part I) a serious explanation of how the distracting clutter accumulated, and then suggests (in Part II) how it can be *not removed* (for it should still be studied on historical grounds), but *shifted to one side*, denoting a non-essential status. This leaves the "heart" of the Good News to be revealed more clearly, and so followed more straightforwardly.

Of course it is likely that this process will be rejected immediately by theologians as being too simplistic, and that devout members of many Churches may be distressed as well, seeing me as disloyal to what they, and I, have been taught throughout our lives.

I am willing to be seen as disloyal, because I place loyalty to Church doctrine as less important than faithfulness to my experience of God. This experience is based intellectually on the story of Jesus' life, but it has recently become more firmly grounded through my personal awareness of God's loving presence both within me, silently, and also within those surrounding me in the persons of my wife, my family, my doctor, my friends and indeed, all whom I meet.

This is not "soppy sentimentality"; it is a simple declaration that, despite selfish instincts within each of us, human beings are basically good. To state this, that we possess innate goodness, one must also acknowledge that selfishness, "looking after Number One," although transmitted through our animal instinct to survive, can descend readily into evil, through our capacity for free-will. We also realize that we, alone of evolutionary life, have the power of "choice" which arises from self-consciousness. The ability to choose is real: to act in a "good" or "bad" way; to "get up" or "lie in bed"; to retaliate or to "make allowance for", which is the beginning of forgiveness, an essential element of compassion. There can be no disputing our possession of this new feature, given to all humanity, nor that it is accompanied by the innate desire to "choose the right" rather than the "wrong" way. It is this desire, unique to human beings, that must wrestle with so many of our evolutionary instincts to try to prevail in our resultant actions.

We know all too well how often it does not prevail, and how disheartened we can become. Evidence of human evil actions in everyday life shows only how difficult it is for such goodness to prevail, but the early Church promoted the idea of "original sin", inherited partly from the Judaistic view of human nature, partly from the misreading of scripture. This was done in order to keep control over its members, by claiming that God's grace, or "spirit", mediated through its members' access to the sacraments, was the only remedy for this "original sin". All those who believe in the compassionate spirit of human nature gradually emerging in us ("humanitarian" is an excellent word; legislation against slavery but one example) can see this error clearly. Today we are conscious of this spirit already within each person, waiting to be set free.

God is well aware of the effect of religious doctrines upon human history, for which we of this generation are only slightly responsible, yet the cumulative effect of which we bear. Moreover, God is not only compassionate, continuing to love us whether we admit God's existence or not, but infinitely patient as well. To God "1,000 years is as a day"[2] so that on God's "third day" we can come at last to realize that human conscience, the desire to "do the right thing," exists as an integral part of human nature, right from birth: God's gift to all humanity.

And there is more Good News. Our self-consciousness has brought us to the realization that there is more to life than mere survival, more even than the ensuring that "the strongest genes pass to the next generation." Questions were asked: "How did life begin?", and were "solved" in primitive fashion in different parts of the world; superstition arose to explain "fortunate" and "unfortunate" happenings together with ways to "influence" whatever, later "whoever", caused them, leading in much of our world to a belief in a Creator God. Considering the shortness of humanity's evolutionary time, we have made remarkable progress, which was shown forth in one person's personal witness that God was not only Creator of all, but had incorporated, literally, within each member of the human race, a part of the Divine Nature. This interior "part", incapable of full description but often termed "Spirit", is designed to work in conjunction with human free will: this is what will ultimately bring into being "the better world" which we desire, described at times as "the Kingdom of God" but without the overtones of dominative kingship as commonly seen to date.

The Good News extends still further. The most salient error of religious organizations is to imply, even to state, that any one of them has a monopoly on knowing and proclaiming God's will; yet there is a second error, pertaining to most religious institutions, which is equally pernicious: it is that membership, through intellectual assent to a descriptive formulation of God's nature, is perceived to carry with it the explicit opportunity for eternal life. Thus, by implication, arises the corollary that those persons failing to make such intellectual assent are denied such opportunity. It is the combined impact of these two proud errors, errors that perpetuate the picture of God as one who separates by judging rather than as one who unites through love, that has turned thinking people away from Churches, to seek life's meaning elsewhere: whether issuing from the lives of others or from their own experience. Instead of considering themselves to be "believers in God" they may accept designations such as "agnostic" or "atheist" while maintaining quite accurately to be "humanitarian". The Good News here is that all persons carry a spirit which is within human nature itself, whether they acknowledge God intellectually or not.

Thus, for each of us, it is a matter of seeking to find the purpose of our life, and also the way to "live out" this purpose to the best of our ability. The answer is to look both outwardly, at the lives of those endeavouring to achieve this goal, including that of Jesus, and inwardly, to a two-fold source of power: our own free-will and our indwelling "spirit", which waits not primarily for intellectual acknowledgment as being "from God", but only to be sought, earnestly, perseveringly and with gradual growth of confidence. It is this combination of strengths that is able to vanquish the power of our evolved animal instincts, those which try to draw us away from our goals, and so often succeed.

You will find that the desired linkage of each person's free will with the "spirit" within is accomplished only through this determination of the person to seek such alignment. The record of Jesus' earthly life clearly shows us how this is to be achieved; so, as you read this book, sweep aside the clutter, and then read the story that remains, which will enable you to follow Jesus' simple, steadfast way – night after night and day after day.

So may the record of Jesus' life be set free from the encrustations that obscure it, and thus reveal what all thinking persons, believers and non-believers in God alike, can now accept to be true: that the goodness of all creation is intended to reach its earthly peak in the relationships of men, women and children with one another. For it is in this quiet, person-by-person way that God's will is done and, through you, God's Kingdom – the "Kingdom" of service to others – truly comes.

And finally, I wish to state that my book is concerned with our present and future world. In no sense is it a mocking, or "putting-down", of the past history of religious institutions. My belief is that the Spirit of Good has continued to exist in human nature from the beginning and thus explains the true spiritual and moral progress made by humanity to date. It is not meant to diminish in any way the great value of such progress made by persons who have been taught that this "enabling Spirit" was given "through the Church" rather than "from the beginning".

On a realistic time scale, humanity has had very little time to evolve. The world's future relies upon those who are coming to believe in the universality of the human "Good Spirit"; it is for the encouragement of such people that I write.

And so, your attempts to live out this wisdom, this awareness of purpose in your life, will fill each day of your earthly life with meaning, and make you willing to leave the matter of your future life in trust, as Jesus did.

If you wish to know the main reason for this book, I suggest you begin with Part Two: The Present, particularly Chapter 8, which recommends the setting-aside of certain sections of the New Testament, the better to concentrate on other sections, thus revealing Jesus' true ministry. The purpose of Part One: The Past is primarily to explain why this is necessary.

Notes - Introduction

1. Nolan 1992, p. 142. For complete book references, see Bibliography.

2. Psalm 90:4 - 'A thousand years in your sight are like a day'. Scripture quotations are from the *Holy Bible, New International Version* (New York International Bible Society, 1984). See Bibliography for complete reference.

Part I – The Past: Obedience
"The Spirit is Within the Church"

Chapter 1: The Ambitious Three
(The Visions of Peter, James & John)

God prepared Jesus for his ministry by setting him in a devout Jewish family in order that in his growing years he would become acquainted with the Jewish religious traditions both officially through worship in the temple and also in the familial manner of God's concern for his people being "told" in the home. This ensured his knowledge of God's truth revealed through certain of the prophets as well as his gradual comprehension of how such truth could be obscured by rabbinical intellectualism which sought to advance one party or another through use of various interpretations, and also to make observance of "God's Laws" by ordinary people more and more complicated and hence difficult.

Upon reaching adulthood, Jesus was moved, with many others, to see the need for repentance as preached by John the Baptist and to seek baptism. It was at this baptism by John that Jesus became convinced that God's relationship to him was real, was familial, was loving and was internal. This was expressed in Mark as Jesus' own recounting of how he had experienced hearing God's voice speaking to him personally from heaven, perhaps using the words ("heaven being torn open" and the Spirit "descending like a dove") as metaphors of his first recognizing his possession of the Spirit. The later versions "improved" Jesus' own account (a) by putting what Jesus heard into a general statement and (b) by turning the dove into "bodily form".[1] From this time, until his death upon the cross, Jesus sought to do God's will through his utterances and actions day by day, finding the inner strength and direction through prayer night by night: he was truly a "Spirit-person."[2]

God vindicated Jesus' ministry in three ways. The first was the most important: to Jesus himself, in prayer, right until his death on the cross. The second way was directed to the world at large: it was to reveal Jesus' ability to heal, to reconcile and to teach through his ministering years; it was also shown in Jesus' steadfast obedience to his understanding of God's will, freely, and even at the cost of personal sacrifice. It was this that came to a climax at the death upon the cross: by the tearing of the temple curtain in two at that moment, and by the inspired cry of the centurion, speaking for all humanity. [3]

The third way that God intended to vindicate Jesus' life was through those whom he had called, that they should continue the ministry that he had begun, their example leading others in future generations to carry on this work. Possibly through the continuing failure of his followers to realize the necessity of giving themselves to more diligent prayer, Jesus came gradually to realize that more was still to be required of him. His personal ministry might end shortly, but they were not to worry because God would enable them, in their turn, to fulfil their own ministries. However, as with Jesus, those concerned were never to be deprived of their free-will.

It is at this point that difficulty begins, for it soon becomes obvious that some of the apostles remained subject not merely to a lack of understanding (as did Jesus occasionally) but more sadly to the pull of human ambition. It has become apparent that although God's ultimate will for the world can never be overturned, it can certainly take many painful detours and be grievously delayed.

Let us turn first to the apostles, the Eleven, from the time of the ending of Jesus' earthly life, on that fateful Friday. We are told nothing about them at this time, but we can begin with some probably safe conjectures. It must have been an extremely difficult time for them. Peter would have rejoined them after his near arrest in the courtyard and they would have lain low, in fear and sadness, leaving the women to view, from a distance, the events as they unfolded. They would have steadfastly prayed and fasted, waiting, wondering, and talking. Undoubtedly the incident when Jesus had questioned them on their understanding of his identity would have loomed large. If, as they thought, he was the Messiah, why had he told them to keep it secret? What great risks for many of them might lie ahead? Were there to be crucifixions for his followers, too?

Such speculations must have led them into not only prayer but intense debate as to what they should do.

And then word reached them that Jesus' grave had been found to be empty![4] What joy, and then what trepidation! At this point, perhaps, Peter, James and John, recalling that they had occasionally been alone with Jesus, might well have been emboldened to proclaim that they had seen a vision during one of such times – a vision which included long-dead historical figures and which, they further claimed, Jesus had forbade them to speak about until after his death.[5] How closely in time the telling of this "secret" vision was to the visions set forth in what are known as the Resurrection Narratives is impossible to know: it might have preceded them as "preparation for" or have followed them as "additional evidence of" the "resurrection appearances" to some of the Eleven. Doubtless these would thus have included Peter, James and John. Indeed, Peter's visit to the empty tomb where he saw the grave-clothes lying,[6] was later to be understood as having been a sighting of the "risen" Jesus.[7] Moreover, within these visions, their risen leader has given them instructions,[8] after which he has again risen, this time into the sky and disappeared from view.[9] Despite the prominence given to these post-resurrection visions, we are not told how many of the Eleven shared in them; the certainty is that there remained doubters among them.[10] (See *Addendum* at end of this chapter, regarding my implication in this paragraph that the Ambitious Three might have fabricated their visions; whether genuinely "seen" or not does not affect my argument).

Now comes the moment when Peter speaks out: he proposes that the apostles be restored to twelve in number.[11] "What is essential is that the number of the Twelve be complete [for they] are a once-for-all symbol for the whole of renewed Israel, never to be replaced when they die."[12]

Even though Peter's justification for this is based on quotations from two psalms, neither of which is relevant to the situation,[13] his suggestion is taken up. Whether the fisherman knew as much as Brown is debatable; my interpretation of Peter's action is that it was a testing of his authority, or primacy among the apostles, by means of a matter of apparent importance but little consequence. He succeeded because the other apostles also were beginning to feel that some kind of "structure" was needed, provided they were the most important parts of it.

Man's idea of how to implement God's plan starts to take shape here: first there should be a structure, "The Twelve", to form a visible "authority" base, and only then will come a proclamation from it.[14] The most interesting thing about this "restoration" of "The Twelve" is that Peter quoted from the psalms. In all three synoptic gospels Jesus promises, in effect, that all who leave possessions and family for his sake or that of the kingdom of God will receive eternal life.[15] And yet, in Matthew only, there is a tail added to Peter's statement seeking something "special" for the disciples,[16] and an insertion in Jesus' reply to the effect that "the Twelve" will be privileged to judge the twelve tribes of Israel.[17] If Jesus had actually uttered this extremely important promise, purportedly imbedded within the answer which is clearly stated in all three gospels, it would also have been included logically in all three; the conclusion is that it was inserted later. Indeed Luke places it more dramatically during the Last Supper,[18] after Jesus has stated that one of the Twelve will betray him,[19] realizing that although there are twelve thrones, at that point there are only eleven followers among those present to whom Jesus is referring. If Jesus had made such a "special promise" Mark's apostolic sources would surely also have ensured that he recorded it, but the earliest gospel is completely silent, on both occasions. As we shall see, in the view of many biblical scholars, there are some passages in these gospels purporting to set forth "words of Jesus spoken during his earthly ministry" that were inserted to strengthen post-Easter attempts to give him Messianic status. These will be discussed in Chapter 3.

The timing of Peter's plan was also important, for the structure needed to be in place before the obvious "time of proclamation to the world": Pentecost, the first great feast after Passover.

There is no reason to doubt that in God's plan, the Good News was to be disseminated both powerfully and joyfully. Nor is there any reason to quarrel with Pentecost being the first viable occasion. The entire account (Acts 2:1-

41) rings true in respect of post-Passion events. When Peter declared "and we are all witnesses of the fact" (v.32b) this might have related only to the discovery of the empty tomb (v.31), yet because it was immediately preceded by the joyful affirmation "God has raised this Jesus to life" (v.32a) the hearers doubtless would understand that what Peter meant was "in a manner visible to us."[20]

However, despite the spirit-led and genuine evangelical fervour of Peter's sermon, one cannot ignore the tone of condemnation: he has turned Jesus' crucifixion into a "guilt trip" for his hearers.[21] There is much of the Baptist's theme renewed here, and so when the people were "cut to the heart" and asked how they should respond, it is no surprise that John's prescription is given: "Repent and be baptized... so that your sins may be forgiven...." It should also be noted that the prescription has been "improved" by certain additions: baptism is now to be "in the name of Jesus *Christ*" thus enabling the sins of those so baptized to be forgiven. In addition there is a very important extended benefit: "And you will receive the gift of the Holy Spirit." This linking of baptism with the reception of the Holy Spirit looks back only to Jesus' own baptism at the hands of John Baptist, and yet Peter states confidently that this will happen to all who are to be baptized in Jesus' name, to which has now been added the title "Christ", meaning "Messiah, the Anointed One."[22]

Jesus did not usually see repentance as being a prerequisite for healing,[23] for the latter was his primary ministry. Although he got very upset when intelligent persons, who ought to have known better (i.e. Pharisees and Sadducees), exalted human tradition over God's commandments,[24] yet he did not consign them to eternal damnation; he still hoped that they would eventually understand. When Jesus did condemn, it was for the single blasphemy of denial of the reality of God's Holy Spirit.[25] Peter, however, had no time for this; he returned to the divisive, Old Testament way of John the Baptist: warn people of the terrible consequences of failing to repent, and declare that the only way to salvation was then to be baptized, thus "joining up" and becoming God's precious "wheat" while those who did not "join up" were, *ipso facto*, "this corrupt generation", mere "chaff". It would be the fire of the Holy Spirit which inspired and illuminated believers,[26] but it would be the fire of judgement-day that would consume those who refused to believe.[27]

The true nature of Jesus' ministry, reconciliation and healing, was at first continued by the apostles. In the early days those who had failed to "join" did not feel threatened; they looked with favour upon the believers.[28] Indeed the enthusiasm of the believers drew many more to join the fellowship.[29] Now, the writer of Acts gives prominence to the ministries of Peter and John, particularly the former. This is not surprising for the gospel accounts give a solid basis for this, in that these two, with their respective brothers, Andrew and James, were the first four chosen by Jesus.[30] Peter, John and James were witnesses not only of the healing of Peter's mother-in-law, but later were chosen, again, to accompany Jesus in the healing of Jairus's daughter.[31] More significant still, at least in the minds of the three, was Jesus' choice of them sometimes to be alone with him when he withdrew for personal prayer.[32] However, despite all three having received their rebukes,[33] their memory of such must soon have either faded or been overladen with other considerations.

It is important to realize that the description of the early fellowship is highly selective,[34] indeed it is "as much a theology of the early church as a history"[35] being written "from the later vantage point of what the author of Acts judges most important and enduring – the primitive community embodying what a Christian community should be."[36] The structure had been established; now it was merely a matter of growth.

Soon the word "Church" will be used for the first time since Pentecost to describe this fellowship. It is the "tale" of Ananias and Sapphira, showing the harsh judgement by Peter resulting in the death of those sullying the purity of the Church.[37] "No story captures better the Israelite mentality of the early believers."[38] The existence of this story indicates that what had been the simple faith in Jesus' healing ministry held by Peter and the others was being submerged by the doctrine of purity. When we read that "a large number of priests became obedient to the faith"[39] we can anticipate how the Church will now evolve. When the first complaints arise, we find "The Twelve" deciding that some kind of hierarchy is required: let there be a lesser ministry of waiting on tables, facilitating their own more important ministry. Even though this is not the actual start of the diaconate as the first step in the three-fold order, it is difficult not to see the simple fishermen taking advice here from the priests recently converted, who were well acquainted with hierarchy.[40]

Despite the title, this chapter contains little concerning the sons of Zebedee, the apostles James and John. It can be safely assumed that they agreed with the direction given by Peter as John is recorded as sharing in healings with him, which resulted in their being jailed together, leading to their joint testimony and in being released together back to their own people, a matter for great rejoicing.[41] Also, they together travelled to Samaria on behalf of those who "had simply been baptized into (or 'in') the name of the Lord Jesus" in order to lay their hands upon them, whereupon "they received the Holy Spirit."[42] One has to assume that the Philip who evangelized those Samaritans could not have been the apostle of that name, because (a) none of the apostles, for some reason, were scattered from Jerusalem during the "great persecution,"[43] and (b) the apostles must have taught that only they, through their laying on of hands, could confer the Holy Spirit else Peter and John would not have made the above-mentioned journey to Samaria. One does wonder, however, if others held this exalted view of the apostles' position. Indeed, the Ethiopian who was baptized by the same Philip "went on his way rejoicing" and did not seem to have lacked anything essential, according to Luke's account.[44]

The manner in which James achieved honour was not one which any person, even an ambitious one, would have sought. He became the first apostle to be martyred, in itself not only a tribute to his eminence but also an indication that both he and Peter were regarded by the authorities as prominent.[45]

Although a new form of religion is emerging, full of spirit-led enthusiasm, and with emphasis upon reconciliation and healing, yet already elements of ritual membership and priestly structure, acceptable to priests, ordinary Jews and to other God-fearers are being introduced.

Addendum to Chapter One: It is important to realize that the claim of certain of the disciples (especially those who were closest to Jesus) to have had Resurrection visions is not one to be lightly dismissed. Caught up with the intensity of Jesus' actions and words during his ministry – one which clearly showed his recognition of his own Spirit within – those involved most probably made this claim sincerely. The burden of my argument really falls upon the way in which these disciples perceived that they ought to proceed as a consequence of the visions: by reverting to the Old Testament theme of "repent or perish", of which John Baptist had been the most recent exponent, indeed the intended last one.[46] They had forgotten that Jesus had warned that this was no longer to be the way. One view recently advanced is that it was to yield to the new, "inclusive way" as practiced by Jesus himself, seen pre-eminently in his many inclusive meals and in his insistence upon the priority of the inner life of the Spirit over external observances. This is vividly brought out by Bruce Chilton in his *Rabbi Jesus: An Intimate Biography*.[47]

Notes - Chapter 1 – The Ambitious Three

1. (Jesus is prepared) Mk 1:10-11; variant (a) Mt 3:16-17; variant (b) Lk 3:21-22. Right from the start of the earliest gospel story, there are "different versions". The first verse of Mark contains the words *"the son of God"* in one fourth-century manuscript; yet these words are omitted in another, also fourth-century. For details of the manuscripts containing the three early gospels (Mark; Matthew; Luke) see Throckmorton 1992, pp. xiv-xix. (For the complete reference for this book, see Bibliography).

2. (Jesus: a Spirit person) Borg & Wright 2000, pp. 60-64. (For the complete reference for this book, see Bibliography). This book , and in particular this Chapter 4 ("Jesus Before and After Easter") (Borg's) deserves careful study.

3. (Jesus: was he "*the* son of God" or "*a* son of God"?) Mk 15:39, see footnote *e* in the NIV.

4. (The Empty Tomb) (Mk 16:1-8; Mt 28:1-8; Lk 24:1-9) Borg 1998, p. 93. (For the complete reference for this book, see Bibliography). "According to the earliest gospel Mark (written around 70), the tomb of Jesus was empty...Resurrection could involve something happening to a corpse (transformation of some kind) but it need not...Thus Easter need not involve the claim that God supernaturally intervened to raise the corpse of Jesus from the tomb." From this I gather that he means that there was some opportunity for the corpse to have been removed in a non-supernatural way, possibly by Joseph, returning after the women had first departed and before the rock was sealed, and hidden away never to be revealed again. Alternatively, as "sealing" and "guards" are mentioned only in Matthew, the stone might not have been difficult for grave-robbers to roll away. I do not suggest that the story put about by the Jews in Mt 28:15 could have any truth in it, nor that either the women or the disciples had any hand in its disposal, but Borg's later words, on his p. 106, note 39, have weight: "Caution about the limits of our knowledge leads me to say that I cannot rule out that possibility, [i.e. God's supernatural intervention] though for a variety of reasons I view it as remote".

5. (The Transfiguration "Secret") Mt 17:1-13; Mk 9:2-13; Lk 9:28-36. For convenience in comparisons of synoptic material, use of a harmony, e.g. Throckmorton 1992 is helpful.

6. (Peter at the tomb) Lk 24:12.

7. (Peter at the tomb, as the disciples understood it) Lk 24:34.

8. (New instructions) Lk 24:47-49.

9. (The Ascension into Heaven) Lk 24:51.

10. (The Resurrection: Reality of the Doubt and Importance of the Doubters) Mt 28:17; Mk 16:14. The attempts to assert that all doubts had been removed were both (a) crude (The resurrected Jesus eats a piece of broiled fish in their presence (Lk 24:42), later expanded to a full breakfast by the writer of the fourth Gospel (Jn 21:4-14) and (b) obviously added later to justify what the Ambitious Three saw as the correct method of proclaiming the Good News (Mk 16:14-18; part of the Later Addition to Mark).

11. (Peter tests his authority) Acts 1:15-22.

12. Brown 1997, p. 282. (For the complete reference for this book, see Bibliography).

13. (Psalms) Ps 69:25; Ps 109:8. The former relates to persecutors (plural) of the psalmist; the latter refers to some hypothetical "evil man" and probably reflects

how the Eleven thought about Judas at that point, although the context is quite different.

14. (Matthias becomes not just a believer, but a Resurrection-witness, chosen by lot) Acts 1:15-end.

15. (The Promise of Eternal Life) Mk 10:28-30; Mt 19:27a (to "follow you!"), 29; Lk 18:28-30.

16. Mt 19:27b ("What then will there be for us?").

17. (Answer to Peter) Mt. 19:28.

18. ("Twelve thrones" for eleven disciples?) Lk 22:28-30.

19. (Betrayal by one disciple) Lk 22:21-23; Mk 14:17-21; Mt 26:20-24, with v.25 a dramatic addition!

20. (Peter's sermon) Acts 2:14-36.

21. (Peter's accusation) Acts 2:23 and part of v.36: "whom you crucified".

22. (Peter's remedy) Acts 2:37, 38. Re John Baptist's call to baptism, see Mt 3:1-10; Mk 1:1-6; Lk 3:1-9.

23. Two examples are The Healing of a Leper (Mt 8:1-4; Mk 1:40-45; Lk 5:12-16) and The Healing of the Man with the Withered Hand (Mt 12:9-14; Mk 3:1-6; Lk 6:6-11). There are many others. Where repentance did take priority in the healing process, it was sometimes unexpressed, as in The Healing of the Paralytic (Mt 9:1-8; Mk 2:1-12; Lk 5:17-26).

24. (Religious traditions vs. God's commandments) Mt 15:1-8; Mk 7:1-13.

25. (The Spirit is all-important, to Jesus) Mt 12:31-32; Mk 3:28-30; Lk 12:10.

26. (Mark reports John Baptist's words with no 'fire' but only Spirit given) Mt 3:11b; Mk 1:8; Lk 3:16b.

27. (Matt. & Luke report John Baptist saying 'a consuming fire' accompanies the Spirit) Mt 3:12; Lk 3:17. It may profitably be noted that although Peter adopts whole heartedly this, the Baptist's belief (Acts 2:40), Mark's sources differ here significantly from those of the other two.

28. (Unbelievers and the "new believers" remain in harmony) Acts 2:47a.

29. (Some unbelievers are gradually "won over") Acts 2:47b.

30. (The First Four Disciples) Mt 4:18-22; Mk 1:16-20 and Lk 5:1-11, assuming Simon's partner to be his brother Andrew. Note that Matt. has Simon being "called Peter" before Jesus calls him.

31. (Two Healings: Simon Peter's Mother-in-law and Jairus's Daughter) On the former occasion, Mark places James and his brother John in "the home of Simon and Andrew", but Andrew need not have been present (Mk 1:29-31); on the latter, the presence of only "Peter, James and John the brother of James" is carefully recorded by Mark (5:37) and Luke (8:51) as well.

32. (The "Favoured Three"?) In particular, the episode which became known as the Transfiguration, see note 5 above.

33. (Rebukes for the three) Peter in Mt 16:23; Mk 8:33. James and John in Mt 20:22-23; Mk 10:38-40.

34. (An ideal beginning) Acts 2:42-end.

35. Brown 1997, p. 286.

36. Brown 1997, p. 286, note 19.

37. (Peter's view of his role in the Church: Prosecutor and (Virtual) Executioner) Acts 5:1-11.

38. Brown 1997, p. 291.

39. (Support for a new "institution") (Acts 6:7b) One is reminded of a current aphorism, applicable particularly to those seeking to retain influence: "If you can't beat 'em, join 'em!"

40. (The "Authority" Syndrome) Acts 6:1-7.

41. (John and Peter as prominent among the Twelve, one episode) Acts 3:1-4:31.

42. (John and Peter as prominent among the Twelve, a second episode) Acts 8:14-17.

43. (The Twelve kept safe) Acts 8:1.

44. (Philip and the Ethiopian) Acts 8:26-39.

45. (The fatal prominence of James) Acts 12:1-3.

46. (Jesus' 'kingdom of heaven') Mt 11:11; Lk 7:28.

47. Chilton 2002, Chapters 4 and 5, pp. 64-102, esp. p. 87 (for the complete reference for this book, see Bibliography): "It is what is *within* that makes a person pure" (author's italics) referring to "[Jesus'] well-known aphorism", i. e. "Nothing outside a man can make him 'unclean' by going into him. Rather it is what comes out of a man that makes him 'unclean'". (Mk 7:15).

Chapter 2: He Who Must Control
(Paul Organizes The Church)

In the words of an eminent historian, "Paul occupies the dominant position in the early Gentile church, even to the extent of being called by some the founder of Christianity."[1] Paul's first letter to the Thessalonians is "the oldest preserved Christian writing."[2] That is to say, it and indeed all seven of the epistles considered of Pauline authorship[3] are probably older than the rest of the New Testament canon, including the gospels and of course the Book of Acts.

However, these Pauline epistles are filled not only with convoluted constructions (as any student of New Testament Greek knows) but manifold allusions, often packed atop one another. In the early centuries they proved a fecund source of theological speculation, later concretized into dogma, and so it is my thesis that Paul's educated writings moved the embryonic Church, already on the reactionary, structural path set by Peter and the newly converted priests, further away from what had been declared and "lived out" by Jesus as God's will for humanity.

The words heard by Paul upon the Damascus Road changed his life. However, Paul's message was not about Jesus' ministry of healing, teaching and non-violence; rather, it was derived from that proclaimed by the apostles at Pentecost, i.e. Jesus' resurrection appearances, and from his own conversion, though neither Paul nor any of those with him had made any actual sighting.[4] He dealt with those moved by his preaching in the same way as had been done at Pentecost, i.e. by baptising them in the name of Jesus, and at least in some cases laying his hands upon them, whereupon they received the Holy Spirit and spoke in tongues and prophesied.[5] In addition, as he moved about in the Gentile world, he appointed elders where communities of believers had been established, to whom he could write his "letters of direction", common-sense acts which meant nevertheless a hierarchy of structure, as had the institution of "table-servers" in Jerusalem discussed in Chapter 1 (at note 40).

It is, however, the richness of his letters' language that has engendered the myriad outpourings of intellectual and mystical words over the following centuries, words that attempt to explain God's plan for the world "through" Jesus, by "fixing" the position of Jesus *vis a vis* God in a way far beyond that stated and demonstrated by Jesus himself, indeed a way that has ensured division and strife over religious matters continuing to the present day. It is my personal opinion, based mainly on intuition, that the contents of Paul's letters should not be used to establish any theological point about Jesus. I accept as inevitable that most, if not all, theologians will dismiss my opinion, but I stand by it.

"Next to Jesus Paul has been the most influential figure in the history of Christianity."[6] "Pauline theology is a very large subject to which many books have been devoted."[7] "Scholars are far from agreement on the key issue in Paul's thought... Baur stressed the antithesis between between human flesh and the divine spirit... Bultmann gives the main thrust to anthropology... A concept of salvation-history is seen as central to many... Beker stresses a Jewish apocalyptic context... Fitzmyer prefers the language of 'eschatological' over 'apocalyptic' and speaks of christocentric soteriology... All these have their elements of truth, provided we realize that they are analytical judgments and that *probably Paul never thought out 'the center of his theology'*."[8] (italics mine).

The fact is that, just prior to his conversion, Paul had been "still breathing out murderous threats against the Lord's disciples" (Acts 9:1). How can "This sudden shift of perspective ... (was it really a vision of Christ or the culmination of a psychological crisis?)"[9] be explained? What cannot be denied is the dramatic impact of the conversion experience itself. There is also the vehemence of Paul's insistence upon Jesus' future importance, based not only in his rising from the dead but also as the one who will come as judge in the final days. One can say that the resurrection, in Paul's mind, is a past validation of Jesus' future role as judge of the world. No one can doubt this when reading the most well-known "linkage", that which has been read aloud for centuries as a lesson especially appropriate for Christian burial (1 Cor.15:20-end) which begins "But Christ has indeed been raised from the dead" (the words in the Book of Common Prayer follow the sixteenth-century

King James Version of the Bible, viz., "Now is Christ risen from the dead"). However, for those who have studied the prelude to this lesson (1 Cor.15:1-19), the effect can be spoiled, for when he catalogues the number of those to whom the risen Jesus "appeared" he radically amplifies the gospel record. "The more than 500 of the brothers at the same time" must relate to some group experience of believers that was post-Pentecost, as would the special appearances to "James, then to all the apostles". Also, he quite understandably decides to include himself; how often can a voice conjure up an appearance when meditated upon at length. Then, just before the lesson begins, he condemns as "to be pitied" all who remain uncertain of Jesus' resurrection (e.g. the Sadducees, among others). He goes on to plead that it must be believed because of the certain imminence of the end of the world: "We will not all sleep, but we will all be changed – in a flash, in the twinkling of an eye, at the last trumpet". Imagine the power of these words in the ears of those to whom they were first read! Indeed today they still lift the hearts of those who have been taught that "If Christ has not been raised, your faith is futile; you are still in your sins."[10] Paul is at his most fervent in these passages, but fervency can lead into exaggeration, and exaggeration into error, even when not intended.

As we who live 2,000 years later now know, Jesus was speaking as a prophet, referring to the coming destruction of Jerusalem and the temple, not to the imminent end of the world.[11] Yet that did not prevent learned persons, reading Paul, from making use of his concerns and predictions to include in their eschatology the person of Jesus coming at the last day to be our judge: a concept essential to Paul's "big idea". But Jesus taught that the coming of the Kingdom of God would be from within the individual; it was to be a true conversion, not an escape from adverse judgement. See Chapter 8 below.

However, it is in ascribing a motive to God, the kind of God in whom Paul probably had been brought up to believe, in relation to the death of Jesus, that has done most harm to Jesus' ministry. "Paul's Christ only has relevance through his death and resurrection, a theology presented in his own words in letters."[12] To attempt to explain Jesus' trust in dying on the cross in terms of a God arranging this as "a sacrifice of atonement" for the sins of all humanity makes a mockery of all that had been taught by Jesus: about living in the present day, about human forgiveness of others, about love for one's enemies, about healing and reconciling. For Paul, all this was to be subordinated to the single essential: to believe that God chose, somehow, to forgive everyone, by means of allowing one person to die as a human sacrifice.[13] Most emphatically, it was Paul "who formulated a meaning for Jesus' death and resurrection … yet it is certainly arguable that his own psychological needs defined the distinctive teachings that he preached to his communities and should be central to any study of him."[14]

Now we come to the principal reason for my entitling this chapter "He Who Must Control". "In some ways this [Epistle to the Galatians] has been considered the most Pauline of the Pauline writings, the one in which anger has caused Paul to say what he really thinks."[15] I cannot find words to express this more accurately. My chapter title is a phrase which well describes the dominant part of Paul's nature. Those who are telling the "Good News" of Jesus in a manner that differs from Paul's are to be "eternally condemned."[16] This is very damaging, for it is clearly revealed here that this brilliant scholar, so zealous first in his attempts to persecute Jesus' followers, is now determined even more zealously to spread his own, personal proclamation of the meaning of Jesus' death and resurrection. Plainly he is what some would call today a "control freak"; for he insists, in another letter, that it is his (Paul's) own gospel that Jesus must have proclaimed.[17]

To-day the question should be asked why theologians originally took seriously this man's confusion of what we now know to be metaphor with fact,[18] together with his varied, indeed random, allocation of the terms "the Messiah", "Christ", "Lord" and "God" in so many passages. Why were his outpourings seen as a basis for the transformation of Jesus, a very good, humble man of prayer, into "the Second Person of the Trinitarian God"? Their reasons for doing so will become apparent in future chapters, and will, I trust, come to be seen as understandable then, but indefensible now.

At this early point, I submit that all theology and christology built up on Paul's words, whether in his letters or in his impassioned sermons in Acts, ought to be negated completely, as the outpourings of one so deluded in his conceit as to claim priority over angels.[19]

Paul would probably not have foreseen that his dramatic idea of Jesus' death, one ostensibly arranged by God, in which "he was delivered over to death for our sins and was raised to life for our justification"[20] would eventually result in Church teaching that Jesus was equal to that same God. But this was only one way of taking Paul's words to invalid extremes. Others were to come.

Paul was literate and very knowledgeable of the Jewish religion, and of many other matters, as well as fervent in spirit: all of which helps to explain his determination to "have his own way, come what may". We shall see in Chapter 4 the peril that arose from later intellects working over Paul's words, concerned to justify later ideas that were considered important in their own times. For example, the concept of Original Sin was given added weight through Paul's extended parallelling of Adam and Jesus. I refer not to the rather naturalistic way set out in the resurrection discourse[21] but to his proceeding to make wildly unjustified moral comparisons of "Old Covenant" and "New Covenant" man which eventually led to a Christianization of the Jewish doctrine of the "Fall" of man.[22] This doctrine stems from Genesis and had formed the basis of the Jewish religion's early insistence upon the birth process itself being a punishment for sin, whence it was but a small step to see everything connected with that process to be unclean. "Augustine maintained that by his sin Adam fell from his original supernatural status, and that through human propagation, which involved concupiscence, the lack of grace was passed on to every human being descended from Adam."[23] And so not only did this flight of Paul's imagination give wings three centuries later to Augustine's dreary emphasis upon "original sin" in Christianity, but it helped reinforce the idea that Jesus, if sinless, could not have been born in the same way as ordinary human beings. Thus, his birth must have required a direct intervention by God, as with the original creation of humanity (Adam): thus we have a second "sinless birth" *via* analogy.

Doubtless Paul's Adam / Jesus linking was not the only item to bring Jews to the idea that a "special" birth was required for Jesus. Their religion included a great distaste for carnality in all forms, and women's periodic issues were seen as unclean. With Paul in so many of his letters advancing Jesus' status to the divine, whether intentionally or not, (e.g. in the hymn that he inserted in one letter[24]) and with the Greeks being fascinated that Paul was preaching not about "an unknown god"[25] but about a known person by whom God would "judge the world" and who had been raised by God from the dead,[26] it is surely not surprising that they would come to believe Paul was proclaiming Jesus as "a God with a name". Occasions where he links the words "God" and "Lord" in passages dealing with Jesus are many; in his mind the two are very closely entwined. It was probably inevitable that his evangelizing metaphors would be turned into literal "truths" by theologians of later centuries.

Paul was not only literate; he shared with Peter, James and John the human desire to be prominent in the proclamation of the gospel. Indeed, he arrogates to himself primacy in carrying the good news into the wider world, a sure sign of his "need to be in control", holding up his missionary journeys as evidence, in contrast to those who stayed among the Hebrew-speakers.

In his early letters, his first to the Thessalonians, throughout, and that to the Galatians, in his closing chapters, he endeavours to urge all members of the assemblies to support one another, encouraging and assisting. This is gentle, egalitarian counselling. But there is no denying that he becomes frustrated in being told of continued "fallings away", for his words turn more shrill, even to the Galatians.[27] In his later letters it is in the area of sexual immorality that he lashes out [28] and he moves on to lawsuits, marriage, widows, sacrifices to idols, cleanliness of foods, right down to women's head coverings.[29] His relations with those in Jerusalem may have varied greatly, but in one major aspect they did see eye-to-eye: those in authority in "the

Church" had every right to instruct and pass judgement upon the lesser members.

"Pauline theology" is a morass into which many theologians, over the centuries, have dipped, struggled and in some cases, sunk from view. Here, as one example of its difficulty, is a reflection on a single point of Paul's theology set out in Romans: whether a punctuation mark was intended to be a period or a comma could determine whether or not a sentence of Paul became "the only example in the undisputed Pauline letters of calling Jesus 'God', and the earliest example of that usage in the New Testament."[30]

Paul certainly deserves credit for organizing the Church; indeed his letters greatly influenced the direction of the Church's development. In a later chapter we shall try to see just how much the theology that Paul spawned has affected Jesus' original ministry.

These four principal characters, Peter, John, James and Paul, supported by Luke and the writers of the "Matthew" gospel (see Chapter 3), and of the Fourth Gospel (originally ascribed to "John", see Chapter Four) laid the foundation for the visible Church of today, particularly in its institutionalism, thus replicating previous, and indeed subsequent, religious groups, all with their insistence upon "membership for salvation".

Let us now turn to the first attempts to put on record Jesus' earthly life and ministry, writings set down after Paul's genuine epistles. These are called the "synoptic gospels" of Mark, Matthew and Luke.

Notes - Chapter 2 – He Who Must Control

1. Freeman 2002, p. 106. (For the complete reference for this book, see Bibliography). The entire Chapter 9 (Paul) is worth attention.

2. Brown 1997, p. 456.

3. Brown 1997, p. 6.

4. (Saul's Conversion) Acts 9:3-8. See Chilton 2002, p. 285: the author emphasizes the inwardness of Paul's vision by drawing attention to the mistranslation in many English versions of the Greek preposition in Gal. 1:16, resulting in the phrase "to me" rather than the correct "in me". I was pleased to note that the NIV has the latter

5. (Paul "admits 'believers' to church membership") Acts 19:5-6.

6. Brown 1997, p. 422.

7. Brown 1997, p. 437.

8. Brown 1997, p. 440.

9. Freeman 2002, p. 110.

10. (Paul sees Jesus' Death and Resurrection as God's Sacrificial Act) I Cor. 15:20, 5-8, 19, 51-2, 17.

11. Nolan 1992, Chapters 11, 12.

12. Freeman 2002, p. 106.

13. (God's Sacrificial Act: upon Jesus) Rom. 3:22-26; 5:8-9. As further evidence of Paul's "tunnel vision", note the juxtaposition of what he sees as two of God's attributes: "love" (towards believers) (v.8) and "wrath" (towards those who do not believe) (v.9).

14. Freeman 2002, pp. 106, 107.

15. Brown 1997, p. 467.

16. ("Agree with me, or else!") Gal. 1:8-9.

17. ("In what I preach, I am right!") Rom. 16:25.

18. (The Adam / Jesus Linkage) Rom. 5:12-19.

19. (Paul's self-belief runs rampant) Gal. 1:8.

20. (Paul states God's Reasons!) Rom. 4:25.

21. (The Adam / Jesus Linkage again) I Cor. 15:45-50.

22. (Death through Adam, Life through Jesus) Rom. 5:12-21.

23. This was from Augustine's "reflection on this verse [Romans 5:12]", Brown 1997, p. 580.

24. (The Christological Hymn) Philip. 2:6-11. "Most think that Paul wrote but did not create these lines; ...a prePauline hymn", Brown 1997, p. 491.

25.   (An Athenian Altar) Acts 17:23.

26.   (Paul sees God appointing Jesus as Judge of the World) Acts 17:31.

27.   (Paul's Temper) Gal. 1:6-9; 3:1-5. Then he begins to teach his version of the Good News and gradually calms down.

28.   (Christians must pass judgement on one another) I Cor. 5.

29.   (Numerous directives which must be followed, with more to come) I Cor. 6 to 11, at various points.

30.   Brown 1997, p. 581.

Part I – The Past: Obedience
"The Spirit is Within the Church"

Chapter 3: Wheat of Truth Amidst Weeds of Myth
(The Early Gospels)

The events in the first two chapters occurred before any surviving record of Jesus' earthly life and ministry had been written. Some of his followers would recall many of his sayings, especially the parables; others his actions

(For convenience each gospel is indicated by four italicized letters: *Matt*, *Mark*, *Luke*)

throughout the years of his ministry, and all, vividly, the events from his arrest until his death.

My aim is to show that the earliest record of Jesus' earthly ministry was the one most concerned with those very years, the one entitled *Mark*, ending with Chapter 16, v. 8, i.e. without the tail that was added later.[1] Most scholars agree this *Mark* to have been written first, with *Matt* and *Luke* later, these latter two using material from *Mark* as well as from another source known as Q, together with some contributions of their own.[2]

When the first records were written, they depended for acceptance upon either apostolic authorship or the next best thing, i.e. that they were directly received from an apostle: hence their early ascriptions to an apostle (Matthew) and to two of the apostles' companions (Mark, Luke). Such ascriptions were made even for the last-written gospel (John, an apostle) and for other writings later included in the Canon of Holy Scripture. It is now generally agreed, however, that none of the gospels were written by an apostle. However, at least for these three "early" ones, most scholars maintain that probably each was written by a single person drawing upon recollections of one or more apostles and other followers. The important point is that *Mark* was probably written first and was so acceptable within a decade as to be known and approved as a guide by the writers of *Matt* and *Luke*, despite their being located in different areas.[3]

The most obvious difference of *Mark* from both *Matt* and *Luke* is the omission of both the Infancy Narratives and Jesus' Resurrection Appearances from the first, but not from the other two. *Mark* is an attempt to put on record what the sources considered essential for the primary role of Jesus to be set out. *Mark*'s sources were probably those mentioned by *Matt* in Jesus' first

Resurrection Appearance to the apostles: "When they saw him, they worshipped him, *but some doubted*" (Mt 28:17b). It is this group of doubters, none named, obviously not of the "inner circle" (Peter, James and John), but ones who were concerned that there be placed on record an accurate account of Jesus' ministry up to the discovery that his tomb was empty.

These particular apostles had noted with increasing uneasiness that the role of humble, healing servants of God, as lived and advocated by Jesus, was being replaced by the establishment of "religious communities", their members fearing imminent judgement and so seeking eternal life for themselves. Peter, John and Paul had been spreading the word as widely as possible for some years, stressing "personal salvation unto eternity", while the assumption by James of the title of "bishop of Jerusalem" convinced the doubting group that the Ambitious Three, as well as Paul, were determined to organize, and thus to rule, rather than to serve. Their doubts had been kept to themselves for long enough; here was an opportunity to redress the balance. A calm and ordered account of Jesus' earthly ministry, setting out primarily his healing and reconciling actions, his association with the poor and the down-trodden, and particularly his exhortations to them, all the apostles, not to be rulers but servants: this was becoming urgently necessary. If such a record could be written down and circulated as widely as possible, then the proper role for Jesus' followers could be made known: the role that Jesus had urged upon them, the role that they had been sent out to fulfil and had failed initially, through lack of understanding. All this cried out to be proclaimed and to be lived.

An apostle likely to have been one of these doubters was Andrew: the only one of the first four chosen by Jesus who was left out of the "inner circle", and who never figures in any post-resurrection account. Another was probably Thomas, whose doubts required rather a crude removal, according to the writer of the Fourth Gospel.[4]

Andrew's (let us say he represents the doubters) concern stemmed from the excessive emphasis being placed upon Jesus' visible resurrection by those who claimed to have witnessed it, further accentuated by Paul's conversion experience, preaching and letters. It was hoped that this record of Jesus' earthly ministry, in its fullness, would draw attention to the need for his followers to concentrate first upon the conduct of their daily lives, bringing salvation through healing others rather than seeking their own "salvation unto immortality". The clear implication of Jesus' accepting the manner of his earthly death was that one was to trust in God to the end. God's raising him to life again was to be a matter, not of visible appearances, vouchsafed only to certain members of the twelve, and then to others, even including their former persecutor Paul, but rather, if faith was to mean anything, of continuing trust in Jesus' own way of life, right to its summit: on the Cross.

Entirely apart from his sources' motives, *Mark's* primacy is invaluable in being a "basic document" upon which accretions can be detected both in its own later manuscripts and when adapted by *Matt* and *Luke*.

Let us examine this first-written gospel *vis-a-vis* the other two, first, as to what it contains that either was not taken up, or was modified, by the others, and secondly, as to what was added by the later writers.

An important point in *Mark* not taken up by the others is Jesus' response to the disciples' inability to heal the epileptic boy.[5] First, *Mark* carefully notes that Jesus evokes the father's faith that his son can be healed before effecting the healing; the others record merely the act of healing. Secondly, Jesus' response to the disciples' question as to their inability to heal, is, according to *Mark*, unequivocally, "This kind can come out only by prayer"; but the others ignore this plain-spoken declaration of the primacy of personal prayer, on which all of Jesus' own ministry was based, day by day, and substitute "lack of faith". Of course faith and prayer must be conjoined, else each is barren, as shown in the lesson taught by Jesus using the fig-tree,[6] but it is prayer that sustains faith rather than *vice versa*: it is, and always has been, easier to profess, even to declaim, faith than to persevere in earnest personal prayer. Later versions of *Mark* attempted to water down this reprimand from Jesus by adding "and fasting" after "by prayer."[7]

A further point about healing shows that *Mark*'s sources are more realistic, and therefore more trustworthy, than those of the later two. In a number of healing situations, where the latter state that "all" were healed, *Mark*'s sources record that only "many" were healed. Two good examples are first, at the very start of his ministry when Jesus went on to heal others after the episode with Peter's mother-in-law, and second, when he attracted crowds of people from a wide area, many with diseases, who had heard of his healings. Thus *Mark* indicates a more accurate approach to Jesus' healings, given that the faith of the person to be healed, or of his relative or representative, was, to Jesus, an essential part of the process.[8]

Another event rich in meaningful interpretations is when a rich man confronted Jesus, addressing him as "Good Teacher".[9] Before dealing with the question itself, important though it is, Jesus first challenges use of the adjective "good" to denote himself, responding bluntly and unequivocally: "No one is good – except God alone". All three gospels have the same meaning even though *Matt* does not mention the word "God". This response has caused a problem to some scholars. For example, Brown says that it "is difficult" and admits that although "Christians had to expand it [the term "God"] to include both the Father in heaven and the Son who had an earthly career", yet "others understand it in the opposite direction, [i.e.] I am not God. However, such a distancing of Jesus from God is not a Marcan theme."[10] Yet this verse might not be "a distancing of Jesus from God" in any real sense at all; it is the later, more theologically "precise" definitions that make it seem so.

Now to turn to what was added by *Matt* and *Luke* to *Mark*'s "basic gospel". *Matt*'s and *Luke*'s sources were not only Peter and Paul; they could have included, for example, the apostle Matthew, well able to write down, either "*in situ*" or shortly after, items such as Jesus' counsels of perfection, his parables, the Beatitudes, the Lord's Prayer, and other sayings and events. These might then have formed a corpus known now as "Q" from which both *Matt* and *Luke* drew gospel material.

In addition, however, there are other insertions which were made not by both *Matt* and *Luke* but by only one of the two. Some of these betray significant self-interest in the supplying source. The most ambitious one appears only in *Matt*. At the same time as Jesus had called his disciples together[11] to ask them a very important question ("*Who do you say I am?*") receiving essentially the same answer ("*The Christ*" i.e. the Messiah) as reported in all three gospels, *Matt* is the only one to record that Jesus had then founded a "church" (*ekklesia*) upon Peter (*Petros*) by virtue of his faith being as a rock (*petra*):

> *Blessed are you, Simon son of Jonah, for this was not revealed to you by man, but by my Father in heaven. And I tell you that you are Peter, and on this rock I will build my church, (ekklesia), and the gates of Hades will not overcome it. I will give you the keys of the kingdom of heaven; whatever you bind on earth will be bound in heaven, and whatever you loose on earth will be loosed in heaven (Mt 16:17-19).*

However, it is extremely unlikely that such a portentous statement could have been overlooked by all of *Mark*'s and *Luke*'s sources. Throughout Jesus' earthly ministry this stands out as the only record of his envisaging the setting up of another religious institution and must therefore, at least, be open to challenge. The only other time that Jesus is said to have used the word "*ekklesia*", two chapters later (Mt 18:17), is to justify "church authorities" in reproving one brother of the group who has sinned against another, likening him to "a pagan or a tax-collector", and therefore presumably excluding him from further "group membership". This is an echo of the puzzling reason for Jesus to give to Peter the "keys of the kingdom of heaven" to "bind" and to "loose" (to imprison and to set free from prison? A "binding" through withholding forgiveness of sin and a "loosing" through sin forgiven?) which was seen, apparently, as the most important part of this earthly "*ekklesia*". It is pertinent at this point to note the motive for Peter's reproof of Ananias and Sapphira,[12] so severe that each of them "fell down and died", an incident designed to emphasize "divine punishment of those violating the purity of the early community.... The impurity is eradicated by the judgment of Peter that brings about the fatal action of God.... It is in describing the fear produced by this intervention ["Great fear seized the whole church"] that Acts uses the term "church" for the first time."[13] It is this incident, (whether factual or rumour "put about"), that betrays the desire of this most ambitious apostle to be seen as the one able to "bind or loose", "save or condemn", symbolized by possession of the "keys of the kingdom". This claim is now perpetuated in humour by the innumerable jokes about "meeting Peter at the Gate of Heaven".

The use of keys to imprison and release, the reclassifying of one not obeying the "rules of the church" to be like "a pagan or a tax-collector", i.e. no longer a community member, and the calling down of fatal vengeance from heaven are all obvious travesties of Jesus' authentic teaching. Yet the fact that one of *Matt*'s sources was able to ensure the insertion of this "Commission to Peter", right into the middle of one taken from *Mark*, demonstrates how quickly the idea had taken hold that Jesus' resurrection meant that a new religious organization was to be formed. Not only was it to have its members set apart by an initiation ceremony, it was to meet regularly to attend a special kind of service led by either an apostle or some duly authorized member, and it seemed willing to accept that Peter and possibly other "authorized members" were able to call down divine judgment upon "offending" members. This was due to the priority given to the teaching that, upon the arrival of an imminent event, whether described as "catastrophe" or "final judgment", a common goal would be possible: that of the attainment of eternal life by members of the community in good standing with the Church authorities.

It was not long before other ambitious apostles ensured a further insertion to the effect that they too were favoured similarly by Jesus.[14] But this was not the way that Jesus taught God's loving forgiveness, as we know from many of his parables.

Although Peter might have wished that Jesus' actual further statement made to him: "Get behind me, Satan!"(Mt 16:23), probably not privately but in front of the others, could have been expunged, it was already firmly imbedded in *Mark* (Mk 8:33) and thus confidently used by *Matt*. Indeed, one can speculate that *Matt* resented Peter's insistence upon having the Petrine Commission inserted, and decided, subversively, to undercut the "rock" by himself supplementing Jesus' rebuke, adding in the same verse the word "*scandalon*" to "*petra*", thus having Jesus call Peter "a stumbling block [i.e. stumbling stone, or obstacle] to me".

Let us now turn to an insertion in *Luke* of words not found in either *Mark* or *Matt*, in a very important event, Jesus' final meal with his disciples: The Institution of the Lord's Supper.[15] After Jesus' words "This is my body" (found in all three gospels) we find inserted in *Luke* both a modifier "given for you", and a command immediately following: "Do this in remembrance of me" (Lk 22:19). It is likely that *Luke*'s source for this addition is Paul himself, who would have learned of the practice of the solemn "breaking of bread" in the first Christian communities[16] soon after his conversion, if not before, and who thus described it in an early letter.[17] It is probably true that Jesus saw the breaking of his body and the outpouring of his blood as his own final act in the inauguration of "the new covenant" foreseen by Jeremiah,[18] yet there is no indication that this would involve either the formation of a new religious institution or the observance of some new, outward, ceremonial act. Examining these verses carefully, we find that it is Paul himself who first claims that Jesus spoke the words inserted in *Luke*, and that it is Paul who goes on so confidently not only to record the name of this fellowship meal as "the Lord's Supper", be it noted for the first time in the New Testament Canon, but to set out its meaning as well.[19] So then, it might well have been Paul, observing the simple "breaking of bread" custom, who in his determination to control matters, *alone* concluded that Jesus had actually both instituted and commanded the continuation of this practice.

Indeed, a prominent Christian goes even further: "I am skeptical that he [Jesus] spoke 'the words of institution' over the bread and wine: 'This is my body' and 'This is my blood'. They look to me to be an early Christian ritualization of the death of Jesus, in which the bread and wine of the common meals that marked Jesus' public activity were invested with symbolic meaning."[20] His skepticism exists because "Even though they [Jesus' words above] have double early independent attestation [in both *Mark* and Paul] ... [he is not able] to imagine a plausible meaning for them as words of Jesus."[21] Indeed, *Mark*'s "early attestation" may not, after all, have been completely independent of Paul's words, which had been written at least a decade earlier.

Thus, as we shall see later in the chapter on sacraments, it is Paul's ideas that may have been chiefly instrumental in causing so much division among followers of Jesus. "Differing church theologies of the eucharist have constituted a very divisive factor in Western Christianity...[These passages in First Corinthians] are extraordinarily important as... the oldest preserved written eucharistic testimony."[22]

The inclusion of what are known as the Infancy Narratives (the first two chapters of both *Matt* and *Luke*) can be simply explained. Although these differ in their details, most obviously in that *Matt* has the angelic message delivered to Joseph in a dream, while *Luke* has it to Mary while she is awake, they have similar motivations, depending upon situations which I leave for scholars to continue to debate. The two most likely were, first, to reassure early Jewish Christians that no spot of original sin clung to Jesus as a consequence of an ordinary, human, and therefore carnal, birth of an expected Messiah, and, secondly, to promote Jesus' divine status, initially among the Gentiles and later among all Christians. To attempt to conclude whether the incarnation, as set out in the Infancy Narratives, the Creeds and the two accounts to be discussed in the next chapter (Hebrews and the Fourth Gospel) is fact or myth has been extensively debated; suffice it to say that many of the arguments in *The Myth of God Incarnate*, edited by John Hick (SCM Press, London, 1977) carry considerable weight and deserve wide recognition.

Finally, it is in the accounts of the "Resurrection Appearances" of Jesus that man's inability to differentiate appearance from reality has become increasingly evident.

Both Luke himself, in writing his Book of Acts, and also his sources for the gospel of *Luke*, were concerned primarily for strengthening the faith of those who already believed not only that his tomb had been discovered empty, but also that Jesus had appeared to Peter and various others.[23] In addition, *Matt* records the women claiming to have been confronted by Jesus [24] but goes on to say that not all of the Eleven were convinced of a visible presence among themselves [25] as he ends his gospel. And then, by some unknown person, at a later date, these "Resurrection Appearances", including an upbraiding of the doubters mentioned by *Matt*, were added to *Mark*, forming what is known today to be a rather obvious "tail."[26]

As it is generally conceded that the gospel accounts were written down after the lifetimes of those who were Jesus' contemporaries, they are thus "hearsay" and their trustworthiness depends greatly upon two things: the veracity of those from whom the writers obtained their respective accounts and the motivations of the writers themselves. The anonymous "Q" might have been a contemporary of Jesus, and would have recorded his teachings as accurately as possible. *Matt* and *Luke* were not only written later but were more influenced by events in Acts, hence there would have been more "input" from those whom I call the "Ambitious Three", eager to establish their eminence in the newly-formed Church. In order to be able to proclaim the "Good News" that Jesus had risen from the dead, there must be something more definite, more convincing, more tangible than some women's claim that a tomb was empty: thus reasoned the Ambitious Three. They had doubtless revealed to the others, possibly on the Friday evening or on the Sabbath, their account of what had happened when Jesus had called them apart on that night on the mountain (The Transfiguration and The Coming of Elijah).[27] Alternatively, they might not have done so until the women arrived on the Sunday. One can imagine how what they claimed to have seen when alone with Jesus might have grown in both colouration and content when linked with the women's news. It explains why Peter ensured that he was the one to visit the tomb. One should also note how Peter's first account of this to *Luke*: "Bending over, he saw the strips of linen lying by themselves"[28] compares with what is later recorded as being what the other apostles and their companions understood to have happened: "It is true! The Lord has risen and has appeared to Simon!"[29] There is no way to tell whether this "upgrading" had been deliberate on Peter's part or excess enthusiasm on that of his hearers, but it is obvious that the two accounts do not match.

Again, the incident on the Emmaus road that Sunday evening, told either by Cleopas or his friend, resembles an incident in the Gospel according to the Hebrews (in Jerome, *On Illustrious Men*, 2). It has been considered possibly a later insertion designed to emphasize the importance of the "breaking of the bread" in a eucharistic context.[30] In any event, after the recounting of the events subsequent to reception of the women's news, including Jesus' peculiar "proof" to remove doubt [31] and his speedy departure,[32] *Luke*'s gospel carries on into his second volume, the Acts of the Apostles, which begins with a reprise.[33] Not surprisingly, there is considerable detail added, as well as possible embellishment. There is also an apparent inconsistency about the length of time Jesus was visible to the disciples: "After his suffering, he [Jesus] showed himself to these men and gave many convincing proofs that he was alive. He appeared to them over a period of forty days."[34] Note how Jesus seems to have "ascended" both on Easter evening and about forty days later,[35] the phrase "forty days" meaning usually a substantial period of time.

It is my position that should God's revelation to humanity include the possibility that human life is destined to continue beyond the grave, it would have been given in such a way as to demand always as much trust for each us to accept as Jesus showed when *he* died: *a trust, not a certainty*, that he would pass through death into a new life.

It should be carefully noted that at no time did Jesus indicate that after his death he would return to this world. To offer "proof" of his entering into eternal life by visibly re-appearing upon the surface of the earth would be a "Sign" that completely vitiated "faith". To believe that God plans eternal life for any human being, including Jesus, must require a faith that does not depend upon "Resurrection Appearances" no matter how many nor to whom. When the women go to Jesus' tomb[36] and discover that it is empty "[they] went out and fled from the tomb" (Mk16:8a). Whether they saw one man (Mk 16:5), two men (Lk 24:4), or an angel (Mt 28:2,5) is immaterial, for in each case a vision is involved, not an actual "appearance of Jesus". I accept the "shorter ending" of Mark as the most trustworthy account of what happened on that particular Sunday, with the absence of Jesus' body being God's sole message, to his followers, that death was not the end of human life, nor was The Pit (Sheol). The Giver of life had shown, in a way that would be always incapable of proof, that such life might extend beyond the grave. *Mark*'s statement that the women who received this message "were afraid" rings true. Even though at first "they said nothing to anyone," they obviously did tell the others. That verse (Mk 16:8) is where *Mark*'s sources believed the gospel account of Jesus' life ought to end. And that is precisely where the difficulties begin.

Those who decided on the contents of the New Testament in the fourth century would have had no idea as to when the gospels had been first written. Because they were designed to set out the events of Jesus' life, they were placed before Paul's letters. Today we know that the letters were written before the gospels. It is essential, then, to realize that the contents of some of the gospels could have been influenced in their formation by Paul's ideas. His manifold allusions to Jesus, in particular as "man", "messiah" and "lord", together with linkings of the words "Lord" and "God" would have led many hearers to be receptive to an exaltation of Jesus' stature, as the years passed.

As the gospels took shape, it was probably inevitable that the simple accounts of Jesus' ministry of healing and reconciliation, accompanied by his inspired parables, would be overborne by spectacular accounts exalting his person. Use of a harmony of these three gospels[37] together with recollection of one of my kitchen duties brought home to me just how cleverly, yet how easily, this had been achieved. Green beans need to be "topped and tailed" to achieve their best, and so do these gospels. The "tops", that is, the Infancy Narratives (*Matt* 1-2; *Luke* 1-2) should be cut off, and also the "tails", that is, the

Appearances of the Risen Lord (*Matt* 28:11-20; *Mark* 16:9-20; *Luke* 24:13-53).

It is generally understood that people should accept as true the whole of these three gospels, indeed the entire New Testament (for some persons, all of the Old Testament as well). But there is an alternative: one can focus upon Jesus' adult life, up to and including his death and burial, as the most important basis for discerning how God meant Jesus' ministry, including his death, to have been interpreted by us. In so doing, we work upon firmer evidence. I strongly believe that this alternative now deserves to be considered seriously, particularly in view of the manner in which later generations have handled the conventional way, which has led into so many labyrinths and divisions.

Notes - Chapter 3 – Wheat of Truth Amidst Weeds of Myth

1.   Brown 1997, p. 148: "4. An Ending Describing Resurrection Appearances Appended by a Later Copyist ([Mark]16:9-20). What I have just written above is the majority view: The original Gospel ended with Mark 16:8". (For complete references for all books, see Bibliography).

2.   Brown 1997, p. 114-15: "The basic argument for Marcan priority is that it solves more problems than any other theory". Although he begins his next paragraph by saying "A realistic conclusion is that *no solution to the Synoptic Problem* [i.e. the inter-relationships of the three gospels] *solves all difficulties*" [author's italics] he ends that same paragraph thus: "If one cannot resolve all the enigmas, it is realistic to accept and work with a relatively simple solution to the Synoptic Problem that is largely satisfactory. That is the spirit in which the theory of Marcan priority (as part of the Two-Source Theory) [Matt. and Luke wrote independently of each other but each depended on Mark and on a posited source called Q, the latter being reconstructed entirely from Matt. and Luke] is recommended to Gospel readers. Even though it remains a hypothesis, one should be aware that important consequences flow from accepting it." Brown 1997: In his summary beginning each gospel, he dates them thus: (p. 127) Mark: "60-75, most likely 68-73"; (p. 172) Matt.: "80-90, give or take a decade"; (p. 226) Luke: "85, give or take five or ten years".

3.   Brown 1997, p. 161.

4. (Miraculous Signs) John 20:24-29.

5. (A Father's Faith and His Son's Healing) (Mt 17:14-21; Mk 9:14-29; Lk 9:37-43a).

6. (The Lesson of the Withered Fig-Tree (Mt 21:20-22; Mk 11:20-25).

7. Throckmorton 1992, p. 104, note "L" re Mk 9:29: 4th century manuscripts (Codex Sinaiticus (S) and Codex Vaticanus (B) follow text; 5th century and later manuscripts add "and fasting" (Throckmorton 1992, pp. xiv-xviii).

8. Jesus' Healings (1) At Evening (Mt 8:16-17; Mk 1:32-34; Lk 4:40-41); Healings (2) Among the Crowds (Mt 12:15-21; Mk 3:7-12; Lk 6:17-19). Healings (3) At Gennesaret (Mt 14:34-36; Mk 6:53-56) This last is possibly a single exception as both gospels state that "all who touched him were healed"; however, Jesus might have known in some way that those who touched him did possess the necessary faith.

9. (The Rich Man) (Mt 19:16-30; Mk 10:17-31; Lk 18:18-30).

10. Brown 1997, p. 141, note 39.

11. (Jesus in important discussion with his disciples) (Mt16:13-23; Mk 8:27-33; Lk 9:18-22).

12. (Peter's Mode of Judgement upon Church Members) Acts 5:1-11.

13. Brown 1997, pp. 291-2.

14. (Others Claim the Power of Earthly Judgement) Matt. 18:18 only; the verbs "bind" and "loose" are here in the plural; in Matt. 16:19 they were in singular form.

15. (The Last Supper) (Mt 26:26-29; Mk 14:22-25; Lk 22:15-20).

16. (The Breaking of Bread) Acts 2:42.

17. (The Lord's Supper) I Cor. 11:23-25.

18. (Prophecy of a New Covenant) Jer. 31:31-34.

19. (Paul's Statements) I Cor. 11:20 for the naming; 10:16-22 and 11:26-34 for meaning and instructions.

20. Borg & Wright 2000, p. 87 (Borg's words).

21. Borg & Wright 2000, p. 263, fn. 31 (Borg's words).

22. Brown 1997, p. 538. The entire paragraph is thought-provoking.

23. (Luke's Narrative of Jesus' Resurrection Appearances) Lk 24:10-end (not in Mt or Mk).

24. (Matthew's Narrative of Jesus' Appearance to the Women at the Tomb) Mt 28:9-10.

25. (Doubters Among the Eleven Disciples) Mt 28:17.

26. (Mark's Gospel Receives a Later "Tail") Mk 16:9-20.

27. (The Episode of Peter, James and John, when alone with Jesus) Mt 17:1-13; Mk 9:13; Lk 9:28-36.

28. (Luke's Understanding of the Episode of Peter at the Tomb) Lk 24:12.

29. (Other People's Understanding of the Episode of Peter at the Tomb) Lk 24:34.

30. (The Episode on the Road to Emmaus) Lk 24:13-35. See Brown 1997, p. 261.

31. (Jesus Eats Earthly Food) Lk 24:41-42.

32. (Jesus Ascends into Heaven) Lk 24:50-51.

33. (Luke's Later Account of Jesus' Resurrection Appearances) Acts 1:1-11.

34. (Luke's Later Account concerning the Times of Jesus' Appearances) Acts 1:3.

35. (Luke's Two Accounts Compared) Lk 24:50-51; Acts 1:9.

36. (The Women at the Tomb) Mt 28:1-8; Mk 16:1-8; Lk 24:1-9.

37. (A very useful resource) Throckmorton 1992 – see Bibliography.

Part I – The Past: Obedience
"The Spirit is Within the Church"

Chapter 4: Jesus is Promoted to God
(Hebrews & the Fourth Gospel)

There are two completely anonymous writings in the New Testament, namely, the Letter to the Hebrews and the Fourth Gospel. However, the early Church did not regard either to be anonymous, but believed that each bore impressive credentials: in the second century the former was ascribed to Paul; as for the latter, its own much-laboured claim to have been written by John, son of Zebedee, casting himself as "the beloved disciple" was accepted. (So it is more correctly "pseudonymous"). Such ascriptions of authorship accordingly won places for both within the New Testament canon. It is my thesis that each of these works was composed deliberately to strengthen the evangelizing outreach of the growing Christian communities, one by trying to elucidate, and the other to provide a more solid "gospel" basis for, Paul's already known view of Jesus' nature and role.

Hebrews

Let us take Hebrews first. This document was designed to appeal to Jews, being steeped in Old Testament analogy, as well as Jewish mythology, and casting Jesus as the pre-existent and only Son of God, who worked out salvation for believers in the role of the Great High Priest of the order of the immortal Melchizedek which had been assigned to him by his Heavenly Father.[1]

This letter is not only "one of the most impressive works in the NT" but also "a conundrum."[2] When a scholar can describe it as "a treatise, a sermon and an epistle", all three, its aim is surely evangelical.[3] It is addressed to Christians interested in learning of any Jewish background, its author being "Jewish but with a good Hellenistic education."[4] It was most probably written after the fall of Jerusalem and the destruction of the temple, which may be why the focus is less upon renewal of temple worship and more upon seeing Jesus as "a new departure" by linking him to Melchizedek. This meant returning to tabernacle matters, which had occurred 1,000 years earlier in Israel's history, long before the temple in Jerusalem.

After the opening declaration of the superior status of Jesus[5] readers are given solemn warnings of the consequences of unbelief.[6] Then, before the writer begins his detailed explication of Jesus' role,[7] he realizes just how complicated this will be and interrupts himself to berate those who had been under the impression that they understood what the new teaching was all about. Not in the least, it appears, for the new believer will be required to "leave the elementary teachings of Christ..." (i.e. "the foundation of repentance... of faith in God, instruction about baptisms, the laying on of hands, the resurrection of the dead, and eternal judgment") "... and go on to maturity."[8] If the writer could have known to what extent theologians, liturgists, Church councils, and the papacies of later centuries have read into this last expression ("go on to maturity") he might have regretted it. On the other hand, he might very well have given a cheer, seeing his own "additional doctrine" theme (for that is what it was) turned into one of the earliest instances of the "valid development of doctrine" theory so conveniently useful to those in authority in religious institutions.

Much as I was impressed in my early years by the persuasiveness of the analogies in this missive, later readings led me to feel that here is a very early intellectual, determined to put forward his own way as being essential for understanding just how God and Jesus worked together. From the beginning of his sermon[9] to his final peroration[10] he is writing to "everyone", in the expectation that what he has written will be copied and recopied and thus become "the explanation of the gospel" acclaimed by all. He probably concludes at v.22 of the final chapter, where he ingenuously describes what he obviously considers a necessary contribution to the understanding of the new covenant, as "a short letter". The three final verses could, of course, have been added by the writer himself or by redactors concerned to give it the appearance of a true letter. But there is no opening greeting, because it is "for all", its writer's original goal, which was eventually achieved through its inclusion in the canon of Holy Scripture.

Fruitful indeed have been the contents of this writing, and it is not my intention to enter into the validity or otherwise of its central theme, which is that Jesus embodied Melchizedek, the king of Salem (that is, Jerusalem) who was also priest of God Most High,[11] and was thus able to offer a perfect sacrifice, that of himself, which all previous high priests had been unable to perform.[12] My only comment is that it relies for acceptance upon the extended metaphor of Paul comparing the roles of Adam and Jesus.[13] The raising of Jesus' status, first in Paul's writings and then in many of the later writings which found their way into the canon of Holy Scripture, not least the two discussed in this chapter, set a major problem for later generations concerned to retain monotheism as well, a problem "solved" by man devising the doctrine of the Trinity.

John

Re the Fourth Gospel, I cannot pretend to the learning of those who have written so many commentaries upon it. To me the first point is that its claim as to authorship is untrue. However, those who accepted that its author was in fact John of Zebedee, who described himself as "the disciple whom Jesus loved", ("the traditional second century attribution"[14]) did take it to be true. It thus gained authenticity for its contents, not only in the second century, but also in the fourth century, at the time of "setting in stone" the canon of the New Testament. Once it had been established that John of Zebedee had not been the author, coupled with the lateness of its origin, the veracity of the entire gospel ought to have become suspect, and particularly with respect to Jesus' words.

Most scholars today are of the opinion that the gospel is not by John of Zebedee, nor by any eye-witness of Jesus' earthly ministry.[15] It was probably not written before 80 A.D., at least a half-century after Jesus' death, and "plausibly [by one or more of] a school of Johannine writing disciples."[16] In the light of this, its marked divergence from the contents and style of the earlier gospels ought to have alerted any person concerned to evaluate its truth. Here are a few examples for illustration:

> (1) *The Prologue* (Jn 1:1-18); this is a hymn probably lifted from some other document and adapted to relate to Jesus. "There is an abundant literature on the Prologue."[17]

(2) *Jesus' Mode of Speaking*: The repeated use of the phrase "I AM" to introduce a self-revelation lies at the opposite pole from the words of Jesus in the early gospels. The Greek words are *"ego eimi"*, literally "I, myself, am". I have taken the liberty of capitalizing both words in the English translation, solely to draw attention to this extreme emphasis upon self-status. Some examples are: (a) "I AM the light of the world" (Jn 8:12); compare with *"You* [the crowds; the disciples] are the light of the world" (Mt 5:14-16); (b) "I AM the gate for the sheep" (Jn 10:7) and "I AM the good shepherd" (Jn 10:11); compare with The Parable of the Lost Sheep (Mt 18:12-14): "*Your* Father in heaven [God]" is like the shepherd in the parable. (c) "I AM the resurrection and the life" (Jn 11:25); see *Raising Lazarus from the Dead*, in Example (3) below. (d) "Before Abraham was born, I AM" (Jn 8:58); an excellent example of having Jesus say what the writer believed true.

(3) *Two Miracles Imagined*: (a) *Changing Water into Wine* (Jn 2:1-11); note especially the final verse: "This, the first of his miraculous signs... He thus revealed his glory, and his disciples put their faith in him." (b) *Raising Lazarus from the Dead* (Jn 11:1-45); again, note especially the final verse: "Therefore many of the Jews who... had seen what Jesus did, put their faith in him." But, to instil faith by means of such miracles (different in nature from the "miracles", i.e. wondrous works of healing and resuscitation, set out in the early gospels) was to yield to one of the three temptations to be resisted by the Jesus of the early gospels (Mt 4:5-7; Lk 4:9-12).

(4) *The Last Supper* (Jn Ch. 13 to 17, in their entirety). Here are five chapters located "just before the Passover Feast... [at] the evening meal" (Jn 13:1-2) Although this group of chapters begins with a dramatic episode (Jesus Washing His Disciples' Feet (Jn 13:4-17), one mentioned nowhere else) we find here a long discourse said to have been uttered by Jesus and now repeated by "the beloved disciple". It is as though the words had been voice-recorded, or that a complete script had been provided by the speaker, including his lengthy prayer. The main purpose was to attempt to place the writer's beliefs about Jesus – his purpose,

his status in relation to God, indeed God's entire plan for the salvation of all mankind – into the very mouth of that same historical Jesus. But merely to scan these five chapters is to disbelieve that the Jesus of the early gospels could have spoken them.

We are told that "in the Greco-Roman world, unlike the world of Judaism, human beings could appear to cross the boundary between human and divine."[18] For example, we have the reaction to Paul's healing of a lame man in Lystra:

> When the crowd saw what Paul had done, they shouted in the Lycaonian language, 'The gods have come down to us in human form!' Barnabas they called Zeus, and Paul they called Hermes because he was the chief speaker. The priest of Zeus, whose temple was just outside the city, brought bulls and wreaths to the city gates because he and the crowd wanted to offer sacrifices to them (Acts 14:11-13).

This dramatic episode illustrates "this new cultural context [within which] we can view the Gospel of John. ... Yet while John may contain 'new' details about Jesus' life that are historically accurate his overall narrative is not. John writes for theological effect."[19]

It was no surprise to discover that scholars whose prime task is to evaluate the authenticity of what Jesus actually said and did during his earthly ministry have come to a consensus that in the Fourth Gospel the voice of Jesus has been supplanted "almost exclusively (and perhaps entirely) [by] the voice of the community."[20] When we now realize that this gospel was the last one to be written, at least one generation after both Jesus and Paul, it may well be seen to be the product of reflection upon Paul's letters, in circulation among the Christian communities for twenty or thirty years. Whether the earlier gospels would have had their "tops and tails" added by this time we do not know, but they still might not have seemed sufficiently "specific" to justify the need for finding evidence of divine status in Jesus' earthly life. Only a "new gospel" fashioned to fit Paul's letters would do; and so it emerged, credited to one of Jesus' own apostles, and going to the extreme of raising the status of Jesus to pre-existence with God the Father.[21]

Although this community would have been termed "Johannine" in the belief that it had been greatly influenced by "John's Gospel", it might more properly be called "Pauline" – one which considered that a gospel supporting that missionary's views was needed.

That is to say, this community's view of Jesus has taken over that of Mark's Gospel. When we have come to understand this, we must accept that human attitudes play an important part in articulating such views; we cannot resort to the convenient escape hatch of saying, about any "generally accepted view" or any doctrinal point, for that matter, that it is true because of the unerring action of the Holy Spirit. In the late first century and early second, the scattered Christian communities were concerned to witness to those around them as to the validity and desirability of their faith. The motive for so doing was evangelistic rather than polemic, and there is no reason for ascribing any more dubious motive. It remains only to point out that the writers of both accounts were claiming false authenticity, the former in the expectation of being seen to be Paul, the latter trusting that his (or his community's) bold ruse of claiming apostolic authorship would succeed.

Yet we still find today that these two works are being relied upon to teach theological truth and, in particular, to buttress the idea of the Trinity, an idea which evolved from the divinizing of Jesus, to try to explain how God the Creator enters into "true believers" through the "Divine Person" of Holy Spirit, and will also carry out "the last judgement" at the end of the world, utilizing another "Divine Person", that of Jesus. At a time when it was firmly believed that these two writings were authentic, such well-meaning attempts to enshrine Jesus as God might have at least seemed credible, but not today.

It is right that the clever and intelligent works that are known as "Hebrews" and "The Gospel of John" (or the "Fourth Gospel") should be retained, for their value in studying the early Christian Church. However, I believe that they should not be considered as affording any insight into Jesus' life, ministry or relationship to God.

Notes - Chapter 4 – Jesus is Promoted to God

1. (Jesus linked to the "high priest for ever", Melchisedek) Ps. 110:4; Heb. 5:4-6.

2. Brown 1997, p. 683. (For complete references for all books see Bibliography).

3. Brown 1997, p. 690; a quotation by H. E. Dana, note 18.

4. Brown 1997, p. 695.

5. (Seeing Jesus as God's [only] Son) Heb. 1:1—3:6.

6. (Warning Against Unbelief) Heb. 3:7—4:end.

7. (Jesus the Great High Priest) Heb. 5:1-10.

8. ("More mature" teachings required) Heb. 6:1-2.

9. (The "Teaching Sermon" begins) Heb. 5:11.

10. (The "Teaching Sermon" ends) Heb. 13:21.

11. (Melchisedek both king and priest) Gen. 14:18.

12. (Description of the Perfect Sacrifice) Heb. 7:15—10:18.

13. (Death Through Adam, Life Through Jesus) Rom. 5:12-21.

14. Brown 1997, p. 334.

15. Brown 1997, p. 369.

16. Brown 1997, p. 334. Also, "It is generally dated to about AD 100" (Freeman 2002, p. 129).

17. Brown 1997, p. 337.

18. Freeman 2002, p. 128.

19. Freeman 2002, p. 129.

20. Borg 1995, pp. 21-22. (For the complete reference for this book, see Bibliography) It is important to note (on p. 21) that this need not denote Borg's personal judgement, but that of "a group of scholars [including Borg] known as the Jesus Seminar... [which] began in 1985".

21. (The Claims of Jesus about Himself) Jn 8:49-58, culminating in "before Abraham was born, I am!"

Chapter 5: Temptation to Power
(Closing the Canon, Closing the Mind)

There can be no denying the honesty of intent among all the Eleven and Paul: it was to carry forward what each of them believed to be God's will as expressed and revealed through Jesus. My thesis is that there was a way to accomplish this that differed from that taken by the followers of Peter, John and James, commencing with the resurrection appearances, and of Paul, commencing with his vision on the Damascus road. A justification for this alternative way to carry forward Jesus' mission has been offered in the first three chapters, but before any attempt can be made to suggest how this alternative view can be relevant and helpful to us today, it is important to set out the main path of development in the Christian Church in the succeeding centuries.

Already in the first century we noted how various Christian communities differed in their understanding of apostolic and Pauline teachings, and how those who saw themselves as competent to deal with such differences tried either to smooth them out or to insist that one or other practice was the correct one. These difficulties continued in the following two centuries, and were exacerbated by conflicts with the temporal power as well. Peter and Paul, it is accepted, were both martyred in Rome, and as the see of Rome became more important, so some of its later bishops, among them Telesphorus (m. *c.*127) and Sixtus II (m. 258), shared in this fate, while there were other martyrdoms and severe persecutions of many Christian communities. Yet this did not dissuade Church leaders from attempting to deal with matters they considered important such as the Quartodecimanism controversy (the proper date to celebrate Easter). St Victor I (Pope 189 to d.198) held synods and excommunicated those who chose 14 Nisan instead of the Sunday following; one result was those so expelled forming "a separate church. They survived as a sect to the fifth century"; another result was "an important step in the history of the papal supremacy."[1] Even during the centuries of persecution, the Church at Rome was seen by other Christian communities as eminent, and therefore the counsels and admonitions of its bishops, by virtue of their following in succession to Peter, as authoritative. By the time of the pontificate of Dionysius (259-68) the Roman Church was already highly organized[2] and in the early years of the reign of Diocletian

(Roman Emperor 284-305) "the Christians seem to have enjoyed the tranquillity which had been theirs since 260."[3] But in 303 the Great Persecution began and continued with extreme ferocity, particularly in the Eastern Church, until it was ended in 313 by the Edict of Milan, which provided "that henceforth Christianity, and all other cults, would be tolerated throughout the empire."[4]

What an important century for the Christian Church was the fourth! To read the entry in Cross under "Constantine the Great" is to realize just how closely the realms of "Church" and "State" were starting to interlock. When a powerful ruler legislated for "religious freedom (of a kind)... exempted Christian clergy from the burden of the decurionate ("laborious offices")[5]... ordered that Sunday should become a public holiday... (and) liberally endowed Christian church building",[6] one can expect rejoicing in the Church.

However, there was a price to pay. Before Constantine's toleration of Christianity, various views about Church polity and doctrine were argued about by Christians, quite vehemently, but no one group had the authority or power to throw any other major group out of communion with the Church. Now consider Constantine's motive in officially accepting Christianity:

"he was sent in 293 to the court of Diocletian, the senior emperor, under whose influence he learned the new Byzantine ideas of absolute sovereignty ... Since (his) policy was to unite the Christian Church to the secular State by the closest possible ties, it was natural that even before he formally professed Christianity himself he should be concerned with the internal affairs of the church. ... (he summoned) the Council of Nicaea (and) took an active part... a circumstance which foreshadows the Byzantine theory of the emperors as supreme rulers of Church and State alike."[7]

The agenda for this first Ecumenical Council was to deal with a teaching which denied the full divinity of Jesus. "The teaching of Arius, though condemned... continued to spread and to agitate the masses, until the Emp. Constantine, anxious for the peace of the newly-unified Empire, called a General Council at Nicaea, which met in 325."[8] The Council decreed that the relation between "the Father and the Son" was correctly defined by the word "*homoousios*" and that the word used by Arius and his followers, "*homoiousios*", was incorrect; therefore Arianism was declared a heresy and its followers banished.[9]

One should certainly query the ability of the Council to come to such a fine theological decision, but there is no doubt of the motive: it was to satisfy the emperor's desire for harmony. It has recently been held that Constantine's main concern may have been not only "to ensure that the growing Christian communities supported his imperial rule, but, shrewd political leader that he was, he also carefully maintained his relationship with paganism."[10] Indeed, H. A. Drake says "[Constantine] was far more successful in creating a stable coalition of both Christians and non-Christians in support of this program of 'peaceful co-existence' than has generally been recognized."[11]

More relevant to this book is that the bishops realized that, if Church authority was desirable, then an obligatory creed could be used as a convenient way not only to ensure orthodoxy, but also to deal with troublesome persons. Their views having been declared to be heretical, i.e. not orthodox (correct), they could then be excommunicated and banished. (However, Arianism was not defeated until the Council of Constantinople in 381, largely assisted by Athanasius). In 330, Constantine had moved his capital to Constantinople (New Rome); thus "the political significance of Rome itself was diminished... and (in the sixth century) the decline of the Byzantine power made it necessary for the Popes to assume political authority in Rome."[12] The temptation to add temporal power to spiritual became increasingly difficult for the Church in the West to resist: "it is from the 4th cent. that the Papacy begins to assume its secular importance and the position which it held in the Middle Ages."[13]

However, temporal power was not really a blessing to the Church: even though it could hold territorial sovereignty from the edict of Constantine in 321 "their possession constantly involved the Popes in temporal disputes, which added nothing to their spiritual authority."[14] More important to the

Church than territorial ownership was the new capability to centralize spiritual power. Take, for example, the actions of an early pope, as the bishops of Rome came to be known:

> "'Leo the Great', (d. 461) Pope from 440... he advanced and consolidated the influence of the Roman see... he sought to strengthen the Church by energetic central government... he pressed his claims to jurisdiction in Africa, Spain and Gaul (and) over all the W. provinces."[15]

But one need not recount all the earthly triumphs and failures of the Christian Church over succeeding centuries; for such has been done by historians and theologians many times over. There have been so many of both: the bringing of civilization and education to the West, with recognition of human worth and compassion, yet offset by continuing emphasis upon conquest, both of so-called "Holy" lands in the doomed Crusades and also of converts, notably the forced conversion of the Jews in Spain and the American natives.

After the heady centuries of exercising temporal power, or of influencing it, as well as possessing spiritual authority, the Papacy's eleven hundred years of territorial power ended in 1870. However, once power has been tasted, indeed savoured over many centuries, it is not easily relinquished. And so, to offset the loss of face through loss of territory, the Roman Church promptly took an (apparently) giant step (also in 1870). To enhance further the spiritual authority of the Pope his world-wide infallibility (in certain matters) was proclaimed.[16] Then, in 1929, even territorial sovereignty was nominally restored when the Roman Church managed to regain a small portion of the earth's surface, called Vatican City, within which its leader presumably exercises not only infallible spiritual authority but temporal power as well.[17]

Such attachment to power is not confined to the Roman part of the Church by any means. The Church of England, since the sixteenth century, has clung to a kind of power-sharing with the ruler and government by means of what is called "Establishment";[18] another, one of the Presbyterian churches, has a somewhat similar arrangement in Scotland, although claiming spiritual independence.[19] Indeed, there may be other places around the globe where churches still claim a vestige of temporal power, but if so, they must be of even less political importance than the three mentioned above. However, most Christian Churches today accept that they have no temporal authority, but continue to claim some spiritual power over their members.

The above brief summary of the Church's links with temporal power was not the only important matter to originate in the fourth century; another, of much greater spiritual import, was the decision to lock certain writings into a canon of Holy Scripture, containing both an Old Testament, in order to preserve the Judaistic background to Christianity, and a New Testament, to provide accounts of the life and teachings of Jesus and the basis for the Christian Church itself. In addition to the actual choice of contents, it is the state of knowledge and the attitude of the Church authorities in the fourth century that should be of concern to those of us seeking truth today.

We have already discussed most of the New Testament: in the first two chapters, the Acts of the Apostles and the Letters written by Paul; in the third, the Synoptic Gospels; and in the fourth, Hebrews and the Fourth Gospel. There is no need to deal with the remainder (the rest of the Letters and the Book of Revelation) for they have no bearing upon my attempt to discover the main purpose of Jesus' life. If used only for information about the early Church's life and teaching, they can be useful for specialists in those fields.

Of course there were many additional writings in those early years, some claiming apostolic authorship, others content to use their own names. For three centuries concerns about deciding which writings ought to be considered worthy of preservation had taken second place to actual strivings for survival, in the face of persecution by the secular authorities. But now, with recognition by Constantine, came the opportunity to study these writings and to decide which were worthy of consideration as Holy Scripture. It soon became apparent that there ought to be some authoritative decision as to what was regarded as essential so that this corpus could be set apart for present and future reference, in all matters of elucidation and controversy. Hence, the New Testament canon was settled during the fourth century, at a time when the ability to test authorship ascriptions was more limited than today, resulting, for example, in more epistles being credited to Paul than he actually wrote, and four gospels, each considered equal in truthfulness, selected (some writings, such as one called "The Gospel of Peter", were rejected). Although it had been the Nicene Creed that enabled orthodoxy to be distinguished from heterodoxy, the Church had used many early writings to assist in formulating its contents; it was obvious that these credal affirmations should be seen to be based upon secure foundations; and it was therefore imperative that such foundations be established. Thus, Damasus (pope from 366) "at a Council prob. held at Rome in 382 promulgated a Canon of Scriptural Books"[20] which contained "a complete list of the canonical books of both the OT and the NT... which is identical with the list given at the Council of Trent [1545-63]."[21] This Canon remains unaltered to the present day, being regarded as the sole basis of all Church doctrine by some parts of the Church, and as sharing such basis with tradition by other parts. There was no apparent thought, once the Canon had been selected, of whether some portions of it might be less inspired than others, or even that some portions might be fraudulent, and therefore those who chose it held that each and every portion of it revealed God's truth, and quite probably, in some manner capable of human understanding. Some fundamentalist Christians press this claim to the present day. In the next chapter we shall see how the Church used Holy Scripture, often in conjunction with tradition, to justify retention of early practice and to develop new areas of influence in their members' lives, all in the name of ensuring their personal "salvation unto eternity". This is what spiritual power meant to the Church.

As man's knowledge of the world expanded, scientifically and geographically, the Church found increasing difficulty in maintaining the Bible's literal truth. The Copernican Revolution and voyages of discovery effectively demolished the Church's *Mappa Mundi* world,[22] centred in Jerusalem, but there was great resistance. When biblical criticism in the nineteenth century exposed a lack of authenticity in some books of the New Testament, the Church resisted any attempt to revise doctrines and practice that had been based upon such books. Hence it has lost credibility.

Instead of humbly accepting the need to change, the Church continues its attempts to dominate its members by insisting upon exterior observances (for example, ceremonies of initiation, ministry and worship) and by claiming authority to rule upon secular matters such as sexual customs and behaviour, as the Mosaic law and commandments had done. The Church has failed to accept that Jesus had deliberately condensed all these rules into the two set forth first in the books of Moses: the two great commandments: to love God,[23] and to love one's neighbour (*i.e.* all other people) as oneself.[24] It was Jesus' personal demonstration of how these two commandments were to be applied in the daily encounters of human life that formed his true ministry to us all: our actions are to be lit by internal authority, derived from what has been planted within each of us, regardless of the name by which it is called (by some, Spirit; by others, inner light) united, by our free-will, to our gradually growing conscience, and issuing in our increasing desire to help others. This is, indeed, the design for the growth of true humanity.

In the next chapter we shall see how far these centuries of power, only for a time secular but in many cases continuously spiritual, as well as increasingly ecclesiastical, led to the moulding of the Christian Church into its present form: respectable, visible, and resistant to anything which might jeopardize its self-image, a self-image which many persons regard as irrelevant to their life.

Although Jesus' true mission shines through at many points, it continues to be obscured by the continuing authoritarianism of much of the Christian Church. This is most easily detectable in the Roman Catholic branch because the Eastern Church seems to have chosen a kind of holy hibernation, while the other parts of the Western Church have divided into countless sects, with some still using an apostolic form as a claim to "authenticity" and others glad to renounce old forms, embracing either new ones or none at all.

The decision to "close the book" of Holy Scripture in the fourth century was, at that time, understandable. Sadly, over succeeding centuries, many brilliant brains have been wasted in being forced to wrestle with those "holy words" and the manifold commentaries thereon in order to satisfy the Church's rules. Today such conformity to any "Canon" of "Holy Words" is rightly seen as a constraint of spirit for thinking people. It is time to realize that the human mind is not designed to be "closed" but to be "open" to the spirit within – developing new concepts of humanity's role in the future.

In the next chapter we shall see, after more centuries of "denial", that people are finally coming to realize that "*the letter kills, but the Spirit gives life*"[25] is a saying that conveys a deep truth: that there is danger in forcing any words written by man to carry meanings beyond their power. For any religion to become known as "A Religion of The Book" indicates over-reliance upon the written word, and this includes the Sacred Scriptures of both the Bible and the Koran. In the closing years of the last century, we saw that more and more people are becoming aware of this truth. No longer seen to be limited in its presence to "believers" (as thought by Paul and many others), the energizing Spirit of Good (whether or not described as "Spirit of God") is now being recognized as innate to every person, with important implications for our relationships one with another. These will be more fully explored in Part II – The Present.

Notes - Chapter 5 – Temptation to Power

1. ODCC 1997 (For the complete reference for this book, see Bibliography) p. 1355 (Quartodecimanism), p. 1693 (Victor I, St).

2. ODCC 1997, p. 1413 (Rome, early Christian).

3. ODCC 1997, p. 483 (Diocletian).

4. Freeman 2002, p. 161.

5.   An opinion of their nature offered by Gibbon in the *Concise Oxford English Dictionary* (1991).

6.   ODCC 1997, p. 405 (Constantine the Great).

7.   ODCC 1997, p. 405 (Constantine the Great).

8.   ODCC 1997, p. 99 (Arianism).

9.   "That jot of difference (between the two Greek terms) was finally settled ... more than three centuries after Christ had walked in Galilee. How those Early Fathers presumed to decide, heaven knows. As Gibbon observed, the Emperor Constantine extinguished the hope of peace and toleration 'from the moment that he assembled 300 bishops within the walls of the same palace'", Article by P. Howard, "OK It's Raining...", commenting on *The Times English Dictionary*, (*The Times*, London, March 3, 2000) Section 1, p. 20. Freeman 2002, Chapters 11 & 12, pp. 156-205 provide ample detail.

10. Freeman 2002, p. 157.

11. Freeman 2002, p. 157, quoting Drake; see Freeman's Note 2 (p. 386) listing two of Drake's recent books.

12. ODCC 1997, pp. 1413-4 (Rome, early Christian).

13. ODCC 1997, p. 405 (Constantine the Great).

14. ODCC 1997, p. 1538 (States of the Church).

15. ODCC 1997, p. 966 (Leo I, St).

16. ODCC 1997, p. 831 (Infallibility).

17. ODCC 1997, p. 934 (Lateran Treaty).

18. ODCC 1997, pp. 562-563 (Establishment).

19. ODCC 1997, p. 1322 (Presbyterianism).

20. ODCC 1997, p. 448 (Damasus, St).

21. ODCC 1997, p. 279 (canon of Scripture).

22. The popular name of the Hereford world map, produced in the 13th century and showing Jerusalem as the centre of the known world, P. D. A. Harvey, *Medieval Maps* (British Library, 1991), p. 30.

23. (The Great Commandment) Deut. 6:5.

24. (The Other Great Commandment) Lev. 19:18, 34.

25. (A saying with a full meaning, beyond the thought of the writer) II Cor. 3:6.

Chapter 6: Rise & Fall of External Authority
(Tradition's Deadly Weight)

In the fourth century the Christian religion had become tolerated by the emperor and Church councils had chosen the Canon of Scripture, formulating as well the rigid theological doctrine of the Nicene Creed. Now it became feasible to declare explicitly what the role of the Church should be, both towards its present members, the believers, and towards those who did not yet believe, the unconverted.

The need for every believer to accept both the Trinitarian view of God and the unique Incarnation of Jesus as the Second Person of the Trinity was explicit in the Nicene Creed and demonstrable from certain passages in Holy Scripture. If there were any doubt of the importance of these twin doctrines it would be dispelled by the clarity with which one document divided the "saved" from the "damned": it originated in the fourth century and was known as "the Athanasian Creed". It can still be found in some church pews though now seldom recited by congregations.[1] Its attempted elucidations of these two mysteries are of less interest here than the motivation for it: *"Whosoever will be saved: before all things it is necessary that he hold the Catholick faith. Which faith except every one do keep whole and undefiled : without doubt he shall perish everlastingly.* (it then explains how to think of the Trinity, after which it is stated) *He therefore that will be saved : must thus think of the Trinity. Furthermore it is necessary to everlasting salvation : that he also believe rightly the Incarnation of our Lord Jesus Christ.* (which is then set forth, continuing on to include belief in Christ's coming for the Last Judgement, at which time) *they that have done good shall go into life everlasting : and they that have done evil into everlasting fire. This is the Catholick faith: which except a man believe faithfully he cannot be saved."* Although traditionally ascribed to Athanasius (c.296-373) "At the beginning of the [20th] century some scholars attributed it to Ambrose (c.339-397)."[2]

Thus, all believers were to be made aware that membership in the Christian church was essential to their salvation. Even as exclusion from the church (known as "excommunication") was equivalent to damnation, so obedience to Church rules was the only path to eternal life.

Some of the greatest thinkers of the Church emerged in the fourth and fifth centuries, bringing prayerful and sincere efforts of intellect into play by preaching and elucidating the twin doctrines mentioned above. Such was the richness of the material in the canon of Scripture that many books were thus written. At this point Chapter 12 of Charles Freeman's book *The Closing of the Western Mind* becomes relevant, its title being "'But what I wish, that must be the canon': Emperors and the Making of Christian Doctrine". The author acknowledges that for this chapter he has drawn heavily on a book by R. Hanson, *The Search for the Christian Doctrine of God* (Edinburgh, 1988) because "it provides the fullest account of the tortuous process by which an orthodoxy was eventually established".[3] Hence, although my next two quotations are in Freeman's words, in his own notes he freely admits his debt not only to Hanson but to other eminent scholars. "Now that the doctrine of the Trinity had been proclaimed, scripture had to be re-interpreted to defend it."[4] Thus we find that the tone of these works includes much that is polemical. There is an abundance of argument against other views, pronouncing them heresies, mining the canon for "proof texts" in the confidence that both authorship and content were accurate and true. To give a few examples, Ambrose wrote much against Arianism; Jerome (c.345-420) against not only Arianism but Pelagianism and Origenism as well; Augustine (of Hippo, 354-430) against Pelagianism and also Donatism, together with fifteen books "On the Trinity"! One can see how once this canon had been pronounced "sacred" it yielded veritable libraries of "holy argument", enabling Church authorities to cast out those who differed and gradually to achieve a centralizing of power. "It is now orthodox faith that shapes exegesis."[5] By the sixth century one who was linked to the three above, Gregory I, (the Great, c.540-604), not so much for his writings as for his asceticism and personal humility, became pope. "His pontificate and personality did much to establish the idea in men's minds that the Papacy was the supreme authority in the Church". These four became known as "the Doctors of the Church."[6]

But, of course, Church membership, through baptism, sealed and completed by confirmation, was only the beginning. Equally essential for salvation was continued participation in the life of the Church, and recognition of this led its leaders to develop the sacramental principle. This was, originally, to permit everyone to participate, in some visible way, in the "mystery" of Christ. Augustine "who defined it (a sacrament) as the 'visible sign of invisible grace' or 'a sign of a sacred thing', applied it to formulae such as the Creed and the Lord's Prayer, and such a wide application was commonplace for the first 1,000 years of the history of the church."[7] During this time there were various attempts to classify the sacraments, but it was not until the twelfth century that the list of "Seven Sacraments" first appeared,[8] which was accepted by Aquinas and by the Councils of Florence (1439) and Trent (1545-63).

"The theological significance of the sacraments lies in:

(1) The exhibition of the principle of the Incarnation. By the embodiment of spiritual reality in material form an appropriate counterpart of the union of God with man in the Person of Christ is made patent.

(2) Their expression of the objectivity of God's action on the human soul. The reception of God's gifts is normally dependent not on changing subjective feelings, but on obedience to the Divine will.

(3) As ordinances mediated through the Church, their essentially social structure. They are the means whereby the union of God and man consequent on the Incarnation is perpetuated in Christ's mystical Body of His Church, its members incorporated in Him, and through Him united to one another."[9]

The reason for the extended quotation above is partly because it is succinct but mainly because it brings out clearly the manner in which the sacraments buttress the claim of the Church to be the exclusive way to God. Once Jesus has been proclaimed to be God Incarnate, and to have declared the Church to be His Body, the sacramental principle is made to order for ensuring that all important events in human life require the mediation of Church authorities. Already in place are the methods of initiation into membership (Baptism; Confirmation) and the spiritual elevation of clergy above the laity

(Ordination) with the further hierarchical refinement to ensure that the clergy would themselves be subject to their bishops, leaders of unchallengeable authority due to their being in direct succession to the original apostles.

After initiation into membership, believers found that the rules of the Church interpenetrated most aspects of their daily lives. They were assured that eternal life beckoned, but in the meantime their faith had to be expressed in obedience to the teachings of the Church, with the sacraments forming the basic structure. After being granted membership, they were obliged to attend regularly at the Eucharist, sometimes with accompanying tithings (church "taxation"), and prior to attendance, to make use of the sacrament of Penance. If they fell mortally ill, the sacrament of Extreme Unction was available, a far cry from the healing role practiced and taught by Jesus. And finally, to make up what was considered to be the sacred number, seven, marriage also was declared a sacrament. Even though theologians agreed that this last was one in which the persons marrying each other administered the sacrament, and not the church official, yet by insisting that the blessing of the Church was required, marriage was brought under its control.

The value of sacraments to the Church authorities rested in their power to enforce obedience to Church teachings. In the early centuries, most of the laity were unable to read and had to take the preachings of their clergy on trust. Not only was baptism the way to enter the church, and so possibly to achieve eternal salvation, but for a child to die unbaptized was tantamount to its damnation, at least as perceived by its parents and people generally; confession of sin, with acceptance of penance, brought forgiveness, but failure to confess even venial sins meant penalties, and for serious sin, damnation. Receiving the Eucharistic sacrament brought strength and joy, but non-attendance carried penalties, and carried to extremes, excommunication, again taught as synonymous with damnation, if not re-admitted to the fellowship of the Church.

History shows that, unfortunately, with such real power in their hands, church leaders often misused it, especially when used in conjunction with secular power. For example, the attachment to certain lands as being "Holy" led spectacularly to the Crusades, and to continuing bitter conflicts with other religions, particularly Judaism and Islam. The idea that any part of the earth is to be considered more "holy" than any other is a religious "blind spot" still in existence today. Again, when it became possible for persons to hear the Scriptures in their own language and, after printing, to be able to read their own bibles, challenges to many Church ordinances arose, testing the reaction of Church authorities. Shamefully, the usual way taken was to declare such challengers to be heretics, and to treat them with scorn and contempt. When there were two versions of orthodoxy vying for dominance, one or both parties would often seek the support of the secular power which meant that treatment of the leaders of the party in disfavour (and therefore heretical) could result in imprisonment and, in some cases, even death.

Gradually, from the seventeenth century, philosophers and other intellectuals began to challenge the "absolute truths" proclaimed by the Church. The spread of literacy meant that obedience should not be unquestioning, but informed. The Church, seeking more positive opportunities, began to justify its role. It became more pastoral, with the negative aspects of neglecting Church sacraments being dropped in favour of emphasizing the personal benefits of proper use. "Extreme Unction", for example, eventually gave way to Jesus' more positive healing approach, and this was also reflected in the confessional, in the endeavour to offer helpful counselling rather than merely to impose penances.

Also, many Christian persons who had rebelled at excessive Church authority began to set up their own parallel structures, free of much of the intolerance that had prevailed earlier. The Protestant Reformation meant that many independent Churches emerged, some claiming close association with the early Church, others, such as the Society of Friends, glad to be free of all forms of sacramental nature. The Unitarian Church went further in refusing to see the need for believers in Jesus' ministry to hold that he was uniquely divine. The eighteenth century, with the advancement of science and the awareness of existence of religions older even than Judaism, brought new forces to bear. And in the nineteenth century Jesus' concern for others was dramatically and forcefully proclaimed through the magnificent work of the Salvation Army. One can sense that humanity was gradually getting ready to accept the truth of God's love without the need for mediation *via* an authoritarian and sacramental Church. Yet even these new religious organizations continued to retain some membership rules and rites.

During the twentieth century, there were basically three ways for Christianity to go: (1) the traditional way, to continue to insist that the Christian Church was unique, because of the doctrines of the Incarnation and the Trinity, and therefore superior to other religions; (2) the ecumenical way, to seek to restore the various separated Churches to some outward form of unity, in some cases even undertaking to revise or rethink the Incarnational and Trinitarian doctrines, with the members of such Churches, in the meantime, seizing the opportunity to work together on humanitarian projects; and (3) to admit that God's nature could be as fully revealed through persons other than Jesus, with insights into God's will for humanity being gained not only through the Bible but from other sources as well.

Throughout the twentieth century, part of the Christian Church regrettably chose to remain with the first, being required to see it as God's "first and only" way. This "closed mind" of the Church is best illustrated by "the profession of faith of the (Counter-Reformation) Council of Trent (1545-63) in which a [Roman] Catholic is required to swear that

> 'I accept Sacred Scripture in the sense in which it has been held, and is held, by Holy Mother Church, to whom it belongs to judge the true sense and interpretation of the Sacred Scripture, nor will I interpret it in any way other than in accordance with the unanimous [sic] agreement of the Fathers.'"[10]

Yet this demand that, in exegesis, faith must take priority over reason has been challenged many times over the centuries, even within the Church. Much of the remainder of Freeman's book brings this out, especially in the later writings of Aquinas.

"Aristotle had argued that it was the natural impulse of human beings to 'desire the good'. Aquinas goes further. The combination of this impulse towards 'the good' with the power of rational thought allows human beings to reach an understanding of what is morally right. There is in people an appetite for the good of their nature as rational, and this is proper to them ...'"[11]

But in this respect Aquinas was ahead of his time. In the realm of exegesis, papal authority remains strong today. The result is that the Church has become increasingly isolated and is being forced to rely upon increasingly authoritarian pronouncements, for example, *Humanae Vitae*, the encyclical issued by Pope Paul VI in 1968 condemning all forms of birth control except the "rhythm method", with many of its members ignoring such edicts to an ever greater extent.

Although there was definite progress in what was seen as God's second way, that of seeking ecumenical unity, yet this was frustrated largely by the authorities of the largest Churches, determined to retain control over doctrine and practice. A striking example of this was The Doctrinal Congregation's Note, (30 June 2000) entitled *"Sister Churches"* stating "It must always be clear, when the expression *sister Churches* is used in this proper sense, that the one, holy, Catholic and apostolic Universal Church [i.e. the Roman Catholic Church alone] is not sister but *mother* of all the particular Churches [i.e. all the other Churches]". (Italics in the original). Closely following this came The Vatican Declaration entitled *"Dominus Iesus"* (6 August 2000).[12] These were not only "A public relations disaster"[13] but, both in their militancy of word and also in their defensiveness of tone, were symptomatic of a much deeper uncertainty, one which must eventually overtake any person or organization claiming to possess "absolute truth".

However, such pronouncements of an "exclusive" nature have had their day, centuries ago, and will today only hasten the gradual lessening of their importance in the minds of all persons seeking enlightenment concerning the place of the human spirit in human relationships.

Indeed, in the ability of many ordinary Church members to work together "at grass-roots level" there were great advances. In the secular sphere they began, legally as well as morally, to recognize "human rights", attempting to end discrimination by race, gender or religion. Also, in greatly increasing numbers, they put to one side religious differences and joined other concerned persons in devoting themselves to helping the poor, the oppressed and the despairing in all parts of the world.

The twentieth century was one of acceleration in all secular areas, acceleration in speed, in exploration, in science, in globalization, and also in personal stress, and especially in individual uncertainty. The mainstream religions, not only Christianity, were still insisting upon membership in a visible institution, but there was a significant growth in what came to be called "New Age" beliefs, ranging through the entire spiritual spectrum. In addition, many "Self-Help" books were marketed, catering primarily to the needs of the individual to such an extent that worldly success for many (usually measured in monetary earnings or visual recognition) became the most sought-after goal of life; those who believed this were known as the "Me generation". But none of this could cloak the fact of humanity's widespread and growing uncertainty not so much of the future but of whether the present moment had any real meaning at all. Along with the New Agers came Deconstructionism in literature, Down-sizing and Demerging in industry and Dumbing Down in education. Instant electronic contacts (via "surfing" and "chat-rooms" on the Internet) were threatening to replace disciplined study and thoughtful discussion.

Yet human beings have continued, as always, to reach out; hoping, despite the waning of "religious" forms of hope, to find meaning in their daily lives.

At the start of the third millennium, there are indications that it is time for God's third way to be tried, and for it to succeed.

Notes – Chapter 6 – Rise and Fall of External Authority

1. *The Book of Common Prayer, Church of England* (Cambridge University Press), The Creed of S. Athanasius, "Upon these Feasts [12 named] and upon Trinity Sunday, shall be sung or said at Morning Prayer, instead of the Apostles' Creed, this Confession of our Christian Faith, commonly called the Creed of Saint Athanasius, by the Minister and people standing," p. 27.

2. ODCC 1997, p. 49 (Ambrose).

3. Freeman 2002, p. 392, Note 3.

4. Freeman 2002, p. 201, see his Note 57 on p. 399.

5. Freeman 2002, p. 201, see his Note 58 on p. 399.

6. ODCC 1997, p. 49 (Ambrose); 867 (Jerome); 128-9 (Augustine, of Hippo); 706-7 (Gregory I).

7. ODCC 1997, p. 1435 (Sacrament).

8. ODCC 1997, p. 1266 (Peter Lombard).

9. ODCC 1997, p. 1435 (Sacrament).

10. Freeman 2002, p. 202.

11. Freeman 2002, p. 337. All Ch. 20 "Thomas Aquinas and the Restoration of Reason" (pp. 329-43) is important.

12. *The Tablet*, September 9, 2000, "*Sister Churches*", p. 1206; and "*Dominus Iesus*" (an abridged version), p. 1203-4.

13. *The Tablet*, September 9, 2000, editorial headline, p. 1179.

Part II –The Present: Challenge
Setting Free the Spirit

Chapter 7: The Third Way
(Opening the Mind: The Spirit's Role Today)

In the first two chapters I attempted to establish that the method used by Peter, James and John from Pentecost onwards (leaving the authenticity or not of their Transfiguration and Resurrection visions entirely to one side) may have been driven by the same motive as that which drove Paul after his vision: to bring in God's kingdom by the exercise of power. This was the power of domination, power resting upon the alleged (yet truly believed by those to whom it was proclaimed) commission given by a person who never advocated such a method, nor practiced it, throughout his earthly ministry.

Then, in chapter three there were set out the attempts, successful on the whole, to place on record Jesus' earthly ministry – his teachings on the perfecting of human relationships, his healings, his inclusivity – as contained in the three synoptic gospels, to counter the growing authoritarianism of the communities' leaders, based on their post-Easter visions. It is this record, that of the earthly ministry of Jesus, that is the key for God's third way, the one I believe to be ultimately intended, as we shall see below.

However, as we saw in the next three chapters, it was the explication of the nature of God and of Jesus' role as deduced from the fourth-century "canon" of Holy Scripture which prevailed, and has continued to prevail, right to the present day, despite the new insights of late twentieth century scholarship. Doctrine had been established on the basis of trust that the writings were literally true; when this was found not to be the case, the Church merely closed its mind and continued to seek ways to justify the original doctrine. And so credibility was lost.

The method used by the Church is to claim that all its important decisions made in the early centuries must have been correct, because of the unerring influence of the Holy Spirit. There is of course no rational way of opposing this, for it is a circular argument, viz.,

> (1) In the fourth century the Church selected out of many writings those which were to form the "Canon" of Scripture, declaring this selection to be "Holy", i.e. true;

(2) Within this "Canon" is stated, explicitly, that God's Holy Spirit will guide Jesus' followers, i.e. the Church, "into all truth."[1]

(3) And therefore, all the proclamations and doctrine based upon anything within the Canon of Holy Scripture (e.g. the Birth Narratives, the Resurrection Visions, Jesus' words proclaiming his divinity, Paul's metaphor about the Church being the body of Christ, etc.) must therefore be true. (Sadly, in subsequent centuries, on the basis that the Holy Spirit continued to guide them into "the truth", some Church leaders were powerful enough to "develop doctrine" from a non-Scriptural basis, e.g. that Mary was conceived "immaculately", i.e. unlike any other person; that she went "bodily" into heaven; and that one particular Church leader, the pope, when speaking "officially" about some important matter, was speaking infallibly; to name only those most obviously speculative).

It is, of course, possible that such a view may be correct, but it is not confirmed by so specious an argument. This book is concerned only to point out that twentieth century scholarship has strongly indicated that it is not correct, and to offer suggestions for the future.

This "Third Way", for the third millennium, would evolve from the successful part of the second way, that is, that part in which individuals have worked, sometimes individually and sometimes together, to help others, not only to better their lives upon earth but to aid their awareness of purpose in their lives, which is the prerequisite for joy of spirit. The key to success eventually would be discerned to be faithfulness in prayer, with prayer being defined as constant communication with the Other, called by believers "God", yet always the God-With-No-Name, other than the mystical term "**I AM**".[2] This is the Other, the Creator, who has implanted within each human being, from the time of the first *homo sapiens*, both an immediate and undeniable self-awareness together with what was at first a dim and uncomprehending sense that contact with this Other was possible. At first it was thought mediators were required and sacrifices of animals and humans necessary, but today we realize that this is not so. Each person is able to communicate with the Other directly, and at all times, because the Spirit of the Other is within.

Communication with the Spirit has usually been described as "prayer"; however, a word less encumbered with tradition is "attention". And such "attention" comes about not through God's waving of a flag and saying "Pay attention!" but through each person's intention to find meaning in one's own life. When one *intends* this, one *attends*, that is, one gives attention to the meaning of one's actions beyond the external, convinced that there is a further meaning involving others and not oneself alone, and that the Spirit of the Other, within, will reveal this. That is to say, our steadfast "attention", day in and day out, will reveal God's intention for each of us throughout our lives. This is the witness of those who have found it to be true, in all corners of the world.

Two things remain to be done. The first, for those who believe in the Spirit within them, is to add their own witness to this truth, and so to give hope and confidence to those who have been taught that there must exist an institution intervening between them and God. Such teaching, true as it may have seemed when humans' realization of God's inner presence was less evident, must yield to the full truth, as lived out in the earthly life of Jesus, and also, it must be emphasized, in the lives of many other persons: the truth that everyone can find sufficient inner authority and power to carry out the purposes for which each was made (called by believers "God's will") by using this constant communication with the Spirit of God, called either "prayer" or "attention", day by day.

The second is for both believers and non-believers in God to continue to work together for a better world through mutual affirmation that there is a good purpose in every person's life, and that such confident affirmation is more important than declarations of, and arguments about, God's existence or non-existence.

This can be seen as an overly simplistic solution not only to the acknowledged major problems of world scale (poverty and oppression to name just two) but also to the stress and uncertainty afflicting so many who have talents and opportunity and know not how best to use them. Yet its basis stems from each person's realization that whatever talents are possessed and developed are designed for use primarily *for the good of others*, whether in material, intellectual, social or aesthetic ways. Thus all humanity can work to express love for one's neighbours in a multitude of ways, both great and small, and so discover the secret of human life: that this is how true joy is to be found. We know that there is overwhelming evidence that lives of deep compassion for others have been lived by both believers and non-believers; and so even the "hope" of eternal life, still less its "certainty", ought never to be held out as the *reason* for such a committed life.

The way to submit any particular view is to be positive. The true meaning of human life, whether perceived as a Creator God's plan for revealing the Divine Purpose or as "the meaning of my own, personal life, God or no God", ought not to relate to any one group, or race, of people, nor to any place, or places, upon the earth. Such meaning can be found not only through the recorded history of the Jewish people, that of the classical ages of Greece and Rome, that of Christianity, indeed of all the world's religions, but also through science's dramatic pushing back of the boundaries of knowledge, especially in the human disciplines of biology and psychology with their growing number of offshoots. All these sources form part of the gradual revelation to us of the truth about humanity.

This book is written both for persons who believe in God and also for those who do not. The next two chapters will be of interest mainly to the former group, and they are written very humbly, for they contain views very different from what I had been taught, had obediently believed, and had sincerely taught to others throughout my life. Yet I must write them, for I believe, now, that (1) maintenance of the fiction that the New Testament is theologically trustworthy in all its parts and (2) retention of the sacramental system, both of these being in support of credal doctrine that was formulated by humans other than Jesus, will prove to be the prime reasons for the impending collapse of the mainstream Churches, over the next few centuries.

Hence I urge, first, that the canon of Scripture be marked in such ways that its later, dogmatic, accretions can be separated out, in order that the true way of Jesus will more clearly stand out to be proclaimed, and to be followed, and second, that sacraments now, at last, be regarded as "excess baggage", admittedly useful in the context of the Church's actual development, but no longer to be required of new believers. Those who presently use them ought to use them confidently to the end, but accept that in future, a completely unmediated communion with the Spirit within each of us is the ultimate way forward for peace, harmony and joy among all earth's peoples. After that has been achieved, it is difficult to see how anyone will refuse to give thanks to the Creator, yet there is still such a long way to go. But God is not jealous, nor vengeful, but of infinite love and patience, willing to await humanity's evolution to the point that it becomes universally accepted that to give service to others has an importance even above open recognition of the Divine Reality.

It is also my hope that persons who have not been concerned with either Scripture or the sacraments in the past, possibly due to the perceived attitudes of those who do believe in them, will come to realize that many, many believers are unsatisfied with the present situation, but have not wished to challenge the church on these two fronts so radically.

If we accept that one's own life can have a purpose beyond personal survival (whether such purpose forms part of a divine plan or not) there are three facts of the present time that are undeniable: the first one is that humanity, in general, has become more aware that in one's approach to other persons, human judgement should be seen as both limited and fallible, while our compassion should be both as self-giving and as effectively directed as possible. This is the primary fact, and the others are related to it.

The second fact is that the statement above represents real progress in our comprehension of the importance of each human life, and of our complete interdependence one with another. This is where knowledge of history is both enlightening and encouraging, although it reveals also how far there is still to go.

And the third fact is the corollary of the above, that this progress will continue to evolve further. More and more men and women will choose to do what they perceive to be right, as so many members of the human race have chosen in the past, and yet, as always, there will be strong forces, from both within and without, to make such choices difficult. Over many years insights have been gained, slowly and with both suffering and joy; further insights will be gained for progress in the future: but will be implemented only at the pace humanity chooses. There are many past generations that have delayed humanity's progress towards this purpose, yet others have moved it forward. Each person has a responsibility to contribute to one's own generation, and thus to the future. And only gradually have we come to realize the infinite kinds of ways that one's contribution can be validly made.

When one regards changes from amoeba to more complicated forms of life, going right through to humanity, one factor has recently impressed me: the time-scales of all the other forms of life before humanity seem to be very large, sometimes "millions of years" being mentioned, but humanity's period, so far, has been slight. I recall it being expressed in one vivid way thus: "If the total span of the world's life, since it began, was shown as twelve hours, that is, for the hour hand to move through a full twelve hours, then the portion of that twelve hours that has been occupied by human beings could be represented by the minute hand moving from 11.55 to 12.00, i.e. the final five minutes out of a total span of twelve hours". The point is, we humans haven't been around very long in terms of evolutionary time.

Yet, in that very brief time we have evolved from primitive hunter-gatherers to what we are today. I am not qualified to speak on matters biological but seem to detect a consensus of learned opinion that humanity's prime difference from the rest of the animal kingdom is the possession of self-consciousness. And, further, that this difference has enabled us to write, enabling succeeding generations to learn from their ancestors, and so to progress in matters of survival, socialization, and, let me add, speculation. The first, survival, was of prime importance, temporally speaking, for the instinct of self-preservation was inherited from earlier forms of life, and self-consciousness has aided this process immeasurably. The second, socialization, is still in very primitive form, for example, whether it is better to kill one's neighbour, to forestall his killing you, or to make friends, so that together you can share good things rather than compete for them. And the last, speculation, (within which I include testing and hypotheses) is an extremely varied activity, entering many different realms of probability. These can be mathematical, scientific, philosophical and even theological. And this last is where man's desire to learn from the past has sometimes taken a wrong turning, for some kinds of knowledge are more legitimate for speculation than others.

It is obvious that growth of human knowledge has been gradual, because the ways of acquiring it have only gradually been expanded. At the beginning of the third millennium the rate of knowledge growth is becoming exponential, already far beyond any one individual's capacity to absorb. In the same way, the growth of human wisdom, conscience and compassion should be recognized to be gradual. The Old Testament attempts to set down the world's history as though humanity arrived early, and that little of consequence came before; however now we know this to be a fallacy, as we realize just how recently we have arrived. The ascription of the weariness of human toil and the pain of child-birth to a sinful fall from a time of primal innocence has led to centuries of error in the understanding both of man's true nature and of God's attitude to man, error which in Christianity is seen in the pernicious doctrine of Original Sin, particularly evidenced in ordinary human birth and, for some writers, in the procreative act itself. Progression from belief in many gods to monotheism was an advance in one sense, even though belief in multiple "gods" continued to exist, perhaps usefully in some religious contexts. God is now seen as no longer requiring animal nor human sacrifices; nor as being The Great Prohibitor, with Ten Commandments, nine of them negatively cast.[3] Indeed "all the [Judaistic] law and the prophets", have been dramatically distilled into just two commandments, both completely positive.[4] Truly advances are being made. But man still clings, in religious matters, too much to the past, to tradition, to the simplistic "absolute certainties" of earlier times, such as the very primitive idea that God still plays favourites and is more concerned with exclusion than inclusion. How many parables, let alone Jesus' own actions and teachings, give the lie to such an Old Covenant belief in a "chosen people"!

Within each one of us there are antecedents of millions of years of species-survival-by-reproduction (with protection of the young coming later) and individual-survival-by-strength (with other means such as shows-of-strength-alone and camouflage coming later), all inherited from times before the first human being evolved. Thus it is only to be expected, given humanity's short span of existence, that wisdom, conscience and compassion still remain less developed than such instincts, despite the great strides of knowledge. Perhaps the great blessing of today's ease of knowledge-acquisition will be to permit the turning of human effort, with urgency, to develop further these three unique attributes of humanity. Examples abound of persons who have already done so in one or more of these three "human factors", including some known to each of us personally, and fortunately, the record of Jesus' earthly life and teaching remains, set out for us all to try both to see as clearly as possible and to apply in our own lives the insights gained.

At the start of this third millennium science has become able to "map" all the different genes in the human body, leading to much speculation as to what this will mean for future generations. Yet the precise way in which humanity differs from the rest of creation remains a fertile field of study.

Little lights have shone out of the darkness through the centuries, lights shining in some cases before Jesus was born and in parts of God's world that Jesus' contemporaries never knew existed. With such lights becoming known, people are at last beginning to appreciate them as being all part of God's ultimate plan for humanity: the amazing triumph of wisdom, conscience and compassion over our inherited animal instincts.

Notes - Chapter 7 – The Third Way

1. John 16:13: "But when he, the Spirit of truth, comes, he will guide you [the apostles, to whom he is speaking, and, as the Church maintains, their successors] into all truth". These words of Jesus recorded here do not appear in any other gospel. In Chapter 4 (in the text before the reference to Note 20 and in Note 20 itself) we have seen that some scholars are of the opinion that few if any of Jesus' words that appear only in the Fourth Gospel can today be held to be authentic.

2. (A Being Beyond Naming) Exod. 3:13-15. Note also a footnote in the New International Version of the Bible concerning the word "Lord" in v. 15: "The Hebrew for LORD sounds like and may be derived from the Hebrew for I AM in verse 14".

3. (The Ten Commandments) Exod. 20:1-17; the only positive one being: "Honour your father and your mother" (v. 12).

4. (The Essence of the Old Testament) Mt 22:37-40; Mk 12:29-31; Lk 10:27. These two "great commandments" are extractions from the Old Testament (Deut. 6:4-5 and Lev. 19:18); Jesus is thus (as is explicitly stated in Mt 22:40) carrying out a "winnowing" of the Hebrew Scriptures, much more radical than, yet similar to, my proposal for the New Testament set out in my next chapter, No. 8.

Part II –The Present: Challenge
Setting Free the Spirit

Chapter 8: Winnowing The Scriptures
(For a Golden Harvest)

The apparently ruthless "winnowing" in this chapter is not designed to be negative; rather, it is hoped that it will direct attention to the proper role that Jesus fulfilled in his earthly ministry, through his teachings and his actions; that is why the Fourth Gospel is removed in its entirety, having been and continuing to be a major distraction from such study. In addition, it is to counter the devastating effects that speculation has had when directed upon a manuscript where the author has written solely to advance his own doctrinal theory, or that of his community, hence the removal of "Hebrews", which drew out from Paul's vivid analogies a completely imaginary "action of God". Thus the encouraging and spirit-filled gems of pastoral insight offered by Paul and the other writers of epistles, sometimes as metaphors or analogies but often as straightforward counsels, especially when freed of theological speculation, will be able to be appreciated properly, some seen to be limited to their own time, but others to be of timeless value.

Jesus was a person who had in his nature not only those parts that had evolved from earlier forms of life, but also, some of God's own nature: those parts of God's nature that are required for God's will to be achieved on earth.

I realize that the above sounds something like "two natures in one person" which forms part of the Church's traditional doctrine of "God Incarnate in Jesus". But I believe that it is possible to hold the position that this "high" view of Jesus ought to be held for all of humankind. Indeed, in Jesus' own frequent use of the term "son of man", together with his emphasis upon the dignity of human beings as human beings and upon the solidarity of the human race, it can be held that Jesus' very identity is humankind itself.[1]

That is to say, every human being has been, and is, created in such a manner as to unite the evolved parts, which from the initial creation of life upon earth had related to earthly survival, with part of God's own nature, specifically that part appropriate for enabling human beings to live their earthly time in a completely new way. For the first time since the creation of life upon earth, earthly survival would cease to be the most important thing.

The instinct of self-preservation, recently refined to be expressed as the instinct to preserve the genes of the present generation in the next, would be able to be set alongside an awareness, only gradually emerging, that there is more purpose in life than mere survival.

This "seed" (as a metaphor) of awareness has been "planted" in every human being, but naturally it has found difficulty in growing because of the sheer strength of the other part of human nature, that which has evolved from earlier forms of life. During the long evolutionary period before humanity emerged there were neither abstract concepts nor moral precepts such as "right" and "wrong" or "good" and "bad", for the survival instinct was in complete control. But with "awareness of purpose", which might be expressed in many ways, such as "self-consciousness", those concepts came into being, and humanity began to tread the long road to its goal. The human race has already travelled from tribalism (with no loyalty beyond it) to globalism (in the sense of recognition of our world-wide interdependence) – even though there remain pockets of "stages on the way", and (we now know) in a remarkably short space of earth-time.

It is hoped, therefore, that the second part of this book will be a small contribution towards a better understanding of the role that Jesus has played, and should continue to play, in this whole process. The role traditionally assigned to him for the past 2000 years has been, in my view, devised by men – men who believed that the kingdom of God to which Jesus referred was to be brought in by power. Unfortunately, it has been the earthly concept of power that has dominated almost all branches of the Christian Church. This is the kind of power that seeks to set its followers apart from others and so to control them. Success has been measured in numbers of members and often through alliances with territorial powers such as monarchs and governments.

In order to achieve this, the person of Jesus was exalted to divine status, and once this had been stated to have been necessarily true, it was then found obligatory to formulate the cumbersome doctrine of the Trinity in order to explain God's presence in other persons ("If I'm going to present Jesus as God, making two persons in the Godhead, why not go for three?" perhaps thought the hyper-imaginative writer of the fourth gospel, as he conjured up an extensive monologue for Jesus at his final meal with his followers).

The declaration by the Church in the third and fourth centuries that certain religious writings were to be "Holy Scripture" ("canonization") has had the inevitable effect of transforming them, in the eyes of "People of the Book", intellectuals and ordinary persons alike, into idols.

For the intellectuals, especially theologians, such writings can be criticized, dissected, analyzed, compared and evaluated, yet due to their "canonical status" can be neither ignored nor dismissed. For the latter, selections from the same writings can be used legitimately as "proof texts" against all who disagree with them, whether the matter be of great importance or trivial. This has been the pattern for centuries.

At the start of the third millennium, it is time for this idol to be seen for what it really is: on one side, a collection of Hebrew scriptures, taken *holus-bolus* by the Church authorities to form a background to God's revelation through Jesus; on the other side, writings setting forth happenings after Jesus' death, as well as the later-perceived meaning of his life and ministry, with emphasis upon his death and resurrection. Yet in the centre, surrounded by the above, there remains the plain account of Jesus' life and teachings, to be found in the trustworthy portions of the three synoptic gospels.

One pressing matter today is to attempt to extricate the essential purpose of Jesus' ministry, in the accounts that have been preserved, from the confusing presence of much else. Unless and until this is done, the Bible, regarded as a Sacred Whole, will gradually lose all credibility, because more and more people, not only scholars, know that it contains a great deal that is irrelevant, dubious, and in many cases, misleading, possibly deliberately, possibly not.

This can be accomplished by the removal of the two principal obstructions caused by men's desire for visible authority: the first is that of claiming God's authority to declare a large body of writings to be wholly sacred, through inclusion in a "Canon" of "Holy Scripture" and the second, that of claiming the same authority to devise a number of rituals, called Sacraments, to mediate God's grace to all Church members by a self-perpetuating group of individuals within the Church.

We shall now deal with this first obstruction in a manner that is straightforward and easy for the reader to implement. As it was essential, in God's plan, for a record of Jesus' earthly life and ministry to be preserved for the benefit of future generations, we can still find it, as wheat hidden among chaff, in the field of the synoptic gospels, waiting to be separated, centuries later, by taking up the metaphorical winnowing fork of independent scholarship.

By using square brackets to enclose passages that, as explained in earlier chapters, ought not to influence our understanding of Jesus' role, the parts remaining unbracketed will become more conspicuous, and thus, it is hoped, more concentrated upon for spiritual insight, for moral action, and for academic study. I suggest the use of such brackets, thus not concealing what is enclosed, because such material can explain why the "traditional" doctrines of the church gained such a hold upon those who regarded them as authentic, as well as providing insight into how the Church actually developed.

These are the passages to be **"square-bracketed"**, grouped by subject, to assist in both location and comprehension:

1. **[The Infancy Narratives]**: Matt. 1:1-2:23; Luke 1:1-2:52. See Chapter 3.

2. **[The Commission to Peter]**: Matt. 16:17-19. See Chapter 3.

3. **[The Transfiguration]**: Matt. 17:1-13; Mark 9:2-13; Luke 9:28-36. See Chapter 1.

4. **[The Exaltation of "The Twelve"]**: Matt. 19:28; Luke 22:28-30. See Chapters 1, 3.

5. **[The Institution of the Lord's Supper]**: Matt. 26:26-29; Mark 14:22-25; Luke 22:15-20. See Chapter 3.

6. **[The Appearances of the Risen Lord]**: Matt. 28:9-20; Mark 16:9-20; Luke 24:13-53. See Chapters 1, 3.

7. **[The Fourth Gospel]** (entire). See Chapter 4.

8. **[Hebrews]** (entire). See Chapter 4.

9. **[Revelation]** (entire). Of little relevance today.

In addition, there are occasions where both sayings ascribed to Jesus and also the description of events between his arrest and execution may be either "history remembered" (actual statements and events) or "prophecy historicized" ("post-Easter retrospective interpretations"). The quoted phrases are used by Borg in his illuminating chapter: "Why Was Jesus Killed?" the reading of which is highly recommended.[2]

It should also be recognized that the language of the Pauline epistles is overwhelmingly filled with rhetoric and metaphor; hence construction of theological doctrine from Pauline sources is to be avoided. Nor should Luke's Acts nor the epistles of non-Pauline authorship be so used.

If, in verse four of the ninetieth psalm, we can sing "A thousand years in your sight are like a day", so also, after two of God's "days" perhaps it is time to make a fresh start, trusting that on the third "day" scholarship and intuition, both undergirded with prayer, will at last break the idol of the entire Bible being "Holy Scripture" and transform it into a wheat crop of the field, a field of the writings of men and therefore a crop which requires to be sifted, in order that the wheat can be separated from the chaff. The Church as an institution has obscured, even denied, this need for long enough.

The temptation is to end the chapter at this point, trusting that the reader will be content to set about discerning the man Jesus, his life and teaching primarily from the three synoptic gospels, excluding the bracketed portions (1-6 above). Yet those who have been brought up to see Jesus as God will be sure to say: "What? No Christmas with its Virgin Birth? No Easter with all those Appearances to the Disciples? What is left?" And for all of us who have shared in the joy of these Festivals, we too can rightly ask the same question. For if "what is left" is trivial, mundane, conventional, then truly Jesus' life and ministry ought not to be studied, for one would not expect any enlightenment or lifting of spirit from so doing.

But it is not trivial, mundane nor conventional. The wheat that remains is there for us to reap as a **Golden Harvest**, able to sustain us throughout our lives.

Even in the square-bracketed Infancy Narratives, there is one episode that could be true and therefore give a clue as to Jesus' intelligence: that he was precocious is illustrated in the story of his staying behind at the time of the passover festival in Jerusalem when he was twelve years old, sitting in the temple among the teachers, listening to them and asking them questions.[3] However, the dialogue between him and his parents should be ignored, being designed to buttress previous claims that Jesus was destined to be, at least, "the Messiah"[4].

At the beginning of his ministry, immediately after his baptism by John,[5] he spent some considerable time ("forty days") by himself, apart from other people.[6] There is no doubt that this was when he sought to find God's will for himself, through earnest, sustained personal prayer. The details of this "search for his vocation" must have been set forth by him to his disciples some time later, including his being tempted to express God's will in ways that he came to realize were not what God wanted. Of course, these temptations occurred throughout his ministry, and at times it proved very difficult for him to discern God's will. Being fully human, he possessed as much of the animal instinct for survival as do the rest of us, and it required constant communication with God when such instinct threatened to throw him "off course". His anger at the poor, barren fig tree, even though caused by hunger, ought not to have caused him to curse it;[7] its withering must have moved him greatly to sorrow, seeing it as God's way of first rebuking and then forgiving him, and he did his best to turn the incident into a teaching on the power of prayer.[8] There is more than one example of Jesus' human impatience, once when the disciples failed to understand his words about the leaven of the Pharisees[9] and again when he overturned the tables in the temple.[10] This is as we would expect, because the thrust of his ministry was largely based on his expectation of an impending catastrophe and consequently he felt that there was no time to lose.[11]

Yet this sense of having little time did not in any way lessen his concern for the people he encountered each day. The healings of individuals were his absolute priority, whether they interrupted other matters or not. He would not be diverted. The healings were so great in number that later accounts gave the impression that he healed "multitudes at a stroke" yet closer inspection shows that it was most probably individuals within those "multitudes" with whom he dealt.

When we read of "miracles" being done by Jesus, we must remember that the word may be used in two senses: one was a breaking, or suspension of a "law of nature" thus demonstrating supernatural power, for example, the raising to life again of a person dead for four days and buried in a tomb,[12] and the other, accomplishing what was regarded as an extremely unusual result, for example, the resuscitating of a person believed to be dead.[13] In both kinds, the response would be the same: "*Mira! Mira!*" ("Wonderful!") In those of the first type the wonder would be directed primarily upon the person who "did it" and his action would be a "sign" of his supernatural power; in those of the second, while the person who "did it" would be seen to be "in favour with" God, yet the wonder would be expressed in glorifying God. Jesus' miracles were all the latter kind, for he steadfastly refused to give "signs" of supernatural power.[14] However, because his wonderful works were so frequent, particularly those of healing, he came to be regarded as in such great favour with God that it was inevitable that stories began to circulate categorizing these works as being in the nature of "signs", from exaggeration. Jesus knew from the beginning of his ministry that he was not to exercise it by supernatural power, the kind that broke the "laws of nature" such as casting himself down from the pinnacle of the temple, thus "testing God" to keep him unhurt. It is this undertaking that helps to destroy the validity of the Fourth Gospel with its story of Jesus' raising of Lazarus, in order for those Jews present to "put their faith in him [Jesus]."[15]

This confusion of the two uses of the word "miracle" had happened before, in Israel's history: for example, the dramatic success of their escape from the Egyptians at the Red Sea.[16] For one thing, "Red Sea" is now known to be "... a mistranslation [of] 'Reed Sea' [which] is a marsh to the North of the Red Sea. All serious scholars today would agree that this crossing and the subsequent drowning of the Egyptian army can be explained by the natural phenomena of tides and winds, which were indeed 'providential' for the Israelites. Nevertheless this remains the greatest miracle in the Old Testament."[17] Similarly Jesus' unexpected rejoining of his disciples who had experienced a fearsome night on a stormy sea[18] "may echo the dry-shod crossing of the Red Sea"[19] and might well have "grown" in the telling and re-telling.

As for the "Feedings of the Multitudes,"[20] although the early Church's interpretation of these incidents was that they were "miracles of multiplication" a noted writer holds that one might have been a "remarkable example of sharing... The 'miracle' was that so many people should suddenly cease to be possessive about the food and begin to share, only to discover that there was more than enough to go around.... Things do tend to 'multiply' when you share them."[21] The entire account is worth reading; the same reasoning would apply to both feedings. There is much in the early gospels to show that Jesus would not have wanted his followers to base their faith upon miracles of the type which would involve suspension of the "laws of nature".

And he continued to teach as well. What wonderful parables have come down to us through being preserved in the gospel record. Sometimes he told the story to everyone, at other times only to the disciples; sometimes their meaning was obvious at once, others he explained on a later occasion. But always these stories dealt with the whole human situation. They are so rich in meaning that one cannot begin to describe them here, but their importance lies in their delivering three things: *new ways to look at God, new ways to live one's own life,* and *new methods for implementing those new ways.*

(A) New ways to look at God: a brief summary shows how radical they were:

1. God is never to be seen as vengeful; his love is enduring and never-failing. When Jesus gave us The Lord's Prayer he began with the Aramaic word for "Father", which was the "familiar" form, "Abba"; today some of us would say "Dad". Jesus' society was one in which parents loved their children, knowing how to give them "good gifts" and never considering doing otherwise.[22]

2. God is for all people; no longer will there be a "chosen race", nor any "chosen group". Jesus first resisted this, but was won over by the faith of two people (the centurion requesting Jesus to heal his servant,[23] and the mother reminding him that the dogs ate the crumbs that fell from the table).[24] This development of Jesus' only gradual understanding of God's acceptance of all people shows emphatically that he was human like the rest of us. Now we have come to see that even his heroic feat of accepting God's will unto death has been matched by others through the centuries into today; and there is ample evidence that such quiet heroism will continue into the future also.

3. No-one is ever lost, in the sense of being without God. The three parables: that of the lost coin,[25] the lost sheep,[26] and the prodigal son[27] drive this truth home.

4. God seeks to forgive everyone; no-one is beyond it, except perhaps those who continue to deny the reality of the Goodness of the Spirit within themselves.[28]

(B) New ways to live one's own life: another brief and incomplete summary:

1. Hate is to be replaced by love, even for one's enemies.[29]

2. Lust of the eyes is as real as that of the body,[30] and both can be overcome only from within.[31]

3. Anger and the desire to retaliate are to be replaced by reconciliation.[32]

4. Generosity is to be practiced to limits beyond the conventional level.[33]

(C) New methods for implementing the above: a few useful prescriptions:

1. When giving, give anonymously, or at least, without ostentation.[34]

2. When fasting, do it in a way that will not be noticed by others.[35]

3. When praying, pray secretly, not to seek credit for prayers in front of others.[36]

4. When declaring something to be true, do not swear but merely let your word stand.[37]

One has only to skim the above to realize just how far there is yet to go for humanity to achieve even a small portion of what has been set forth as our goal. And yet Jesus did achieve it, in his lifetime. He did it through living it day by day, and called upon his followers to do the same.

Through his life he stressed the importance of *both* action and teaching. He saw an impending catastrophe and did his best to prepare others for it, within his capabilities. The lesson for us is to follow his example. We are to trust that throughout our lives, by means of our constant communication with our Good Spirit within, whether we term it "prayer", "giving attention" or "enlightening our conscience", we shall achieve, day by day (and with many failures along the way, all forgiven) our part in bringing forward humanity to its proper end, no matter how many centuries or millennia distant that may be. That is what Jesus always strove to do. As he perished on the cross, he was reciting the psalms, and I believe his closing words, "*My God, my God, why have you forsaken me?*"[38] and then a few moments later, after he had been offered a drink, "*Father, into your hands I commit my spirit*"[39] expressed what every one of us will feel as we die: both doubt and trust, intermingled to the last in one's mind, but with the latter *always* prevailing in one's heart. Jesus not only recognized his spirit within, but that he could commit it to God as he died: trusting it into his Creator's loving care. And for the many of us who may not be given opportunity at our moment of death so to reflect and to commit, I believe that God accepts us all, in a perfect melding of love and justice.

It is true that the early gospels record occasions when Jesus spoke of the future, and of rising again; three times he declared his impending passion and that he would rise again. After all he disagreed with the Sadducees about their belief that there would be no resurrection. Why should he not follow the Pharisees in believing in a resurrection? Perhaps in his early ministry he did see himself as the "anointed one" destined to fulfil a special role in revealing both God's nature, so far as required for humanity to know, and also how to work out God's will in our lives; if so, he would have seen no harm in encouraging his followers so to believe. It was when he came to realize that the Judaistic idea, and therefore that of his followers, might involve violence, because they saw "Messiah" as a conquering king, that he ceased to maintain it, though he could not deny that, in a real sense, he was "*an* anointed one", but not as they understood it. As for the phrase "after three days",

> "this is merely a Hebrew and Aramaic way of saying 'soon' or 'not long afterwards'. Most Jews at the time believed in the resurrection of the dead on the last day, and of all Jews the martyrs were most assured of rising on that day. Jesus could not have predicted that he would rise before the last day, otherwise all the confusion, doubt and surprise when he did rise would make no sense at all. In other words, all that this 'prediction' could mean is that Jesus as a kind of prophet-martyr expected to rise again on the last day *and* that the last day would

come soon.... [Jesus] never raises the matter [of the resurrection] of his own accord.... We may therefore wonder whether Jesus did in fact make any 'resurrection predictions'.... This is not to say that Jesus did not believe in the resurrection. He no doubt believed in it along with many other things that the Jews of his time believed in;... For Jesus, in his time, resurrection... was simply not the issue."[40]

It is no part of this book to attempt to write a full account of the importance of Jesus to the world. Very briefly have I attempted, first, to separate out the misleading "chaff" by means of square-bracketing six sections in the early gospels and three other books of the New Testament. Then I highlighted a few aspects of the "good wheat" that remains. Further study of these early gospels will reveal still more fruitful treasures: there are Jesus' teachings, especially in the "Sermon on the Mount" (Mt 5:1-29) and the "Sermon on the Plain" (Lk 6:20-49), which are collections of Jesus' cogent but brief sayings probably uttered many times during his ministry, and not, as the titles suggest, two long sermons. There are also Jesus' masterful ways of putting these teachings into practice through his healings and his innovative "inclusive meals", together with his presentation of their essence by means of parables, encouraging his hearers to think for themselves.

Do not think that we shall leave Christmas behind; it shall be kept with joy as the Birthday of Jesus, who came to reveal to us that the Spirit of God (for those of you reluctant to believe in God, then the undeniable Spirit of *Good*) resides in each one of us, alongside our free-will. And even as we give thanks for the good actions of persons today in their obituaries and at their memorial services, we shall continue also to remember the anniversary of Jesus' death as the day on which a noble human life was offered to God, in the firm trust that he had endeavoured to do God's will (that which is "right") in all his decisions, and that therefore he died, although in agony yet content in a life fulfilled – a truly "Good Friday". Even Easter Day can continue to be celebrated, by those of us who share Jesus' belief in the resurrection of the person, as being the most hopeful consequence of trusting in God's loving care that one can imagine, recognizing at the same time that this joy is based on sheer trust (Jesus' and our own), and not on fact. Others have the right to hold to different ideas about how matters unfold after death, neither lessening their appreciation for what Jesus' accomplished in his earthly life nor forfeiting God's continuing love for them.

The next chapter will concentrate on showing why the traditional belief that God's purpose for us is best revealed through the authority of an institution is no longer tenable. And then the final chapter will attempt to show that the following of Jesus' way will today entail the gradual development in each person of what is called "the 'Abba-experience': [Jesus'] unique experience of intimate closeness to God."[41] Jesus' own personal experience was unique, but God's existence within, through the indwelling Spirit, as we become more fully aware of it, will result in an experience both unique and encouraging, for each one of us, to sustain us throughout our life.

Notes - Chapter 8 – Winnowing the Scriptures

1. Nolan 1992, p. 146. For complete book references, see Bibliography.

2. Borg & Wright 2000, pp. 79-91.

3. (The Boy Jesus at the Temple) Lk 2:41-46. Cf Lk 2:40.

4. (Israel's Great Expectation) Lk 2:10, 26, 38.

5. (The Baptism of Jesus): Mt 3:13-17; Mk 1:9-11; Lk 3:21-22.

6. (The Temptation): Mt 4:1-11; Mk 1:12-13; Lk 4:1-13.

7. (The Cursing of the Fig Tree): Mt 21:18-19; Mk 11:12-14.

8. (The Lesson from the Withered Fig Tree): Mt 21:20-22; Mk 11: 20-25.

9. (The Yeast of the Pharisees): Mt 16:5-12; Mk 8:14-21.

10. (Cleansing of the Temple): Mt 21:10-17; Mk 11:11, 15-19;Lk 19:45-48.

11. Nolan 1992, pp. 21-22, 104.

12. (The Lazarus Episode) John 11:1-44, esp. vv. 14, 25, 43-44.

13. (Jairus' Daughter) Mt 9:18-19, 23-25; Mk 5:22-24, 35-43; Lk 8:41-42, 49-56.

14. (Signs): Mt 12:38-42, 16:1-4; Mk 8:11-13; Lk 11:29-32.

15. (Would Jesus test God to win people's belief?) John 11:45. See 'The Temptation' note 6 above.

16. (Benefit of Scholarship) Exod. ch. 14.

17. Nolan 1992, pp. 41-42.

18. (The Walking on the Water): Mt 14:22-33; Mk 6:45-52.

19. Brown 1997, p. 136.

20. (Feeding of 5,000): Mt 14:13-21; Mk 6:30-44; Lk 9:10-17; and (Feeding of 4,000): Mt 15:32-29; Mk 8:1-10.

21. Nolan 1992, p. 64.

22. (Good Parents) Mt 7:9-11; Lk 11:11-13.

23. (The Centurion's Faith) Mt 8:5-13; Lk 7:1-10.

24. (Faith Beyond Israel) Mt 15:22-28; Mk 7:25-30.

25. (The Lost Coin) Lk 15:8-10.

26. (The Lost Sheep) Mt 18:12-14; Lk 15:4-7.

27. (The Prodigal Son) Lk 15:11-32.

28. (Forgiveness) Mt 12:31-32; Mk 3:28-30; Lk 12:10.

29. (Love for Enemies) Mt 5:43-48; Lk 6:27-28, 32-36.

30. (Where Danger of Sin Begins: 'Inside') Mt 5:27-28.

31. (Actions Speak Louder Than Words) Mt 7:16-21, 12:33-35; Lk 6:43-46.

32. (Be Quick to 'Make Up') Mt 5:21-24, 38-39; Lk 6:29a.

33. (As Compassion deepens, Generosity will grow) Mt 5:40-42; Lk 6:29b-30.

34. (Where Real Joy begins: 'Inside') Mt 6:1-4.

35. (Controlling our Desires begins 'Inside') Mt 6:16-18.

36. (Where Prayer begins: 'Inside') Mt 6:5-8.

37. ('Giving Your Word') Mt 5:33-37.

38.   (Psalm 22:1) Mt 27:46; Mk 15:34.

39.   (Psalm 31:5) Lk 23:46

40.   Nolan 1992, p. 142.

41.   Nolan 1992, p. 151.

Part II – The Present: Challenge
Setting Free the Spirit

Chapter 9: The Obsolete Seven
(Sacraments: From Helps to Hindrances)

Having in the earlier chapters offered an explanation as to why the Church came to be set up, and continues to exist today, I must admit that I have no idea how things would have worked out had my alternative view prevailed at the time of Jesus' death. I take refuge in maintaining that God's will is never circumvented, and acknowledging that these last two thousand years have seen Jesus' life and ministry made known throughout the whole world. Unfortunately, accompanying this "Good News" was the power structure devised by the wit of man which is now recognized as the albatross around its neck. The claim to the uniqueness of Jesus by exalting him to god-status has been recognized by sufficient scholars as being an early error;[1] what remains is for honest admission that God's grace has always and everywhere existed within humanity, and thus has emerged in individual lives over the whole span of human life on this planet.

As the chapter title indicates, a first step is one that has already been taken by an increasing number of thinking people: it is to free moral progress from dependence upon institutional religion. Borg's masterful perceptions of Jesus living out his earthly ministry are categorized under types of religious personality, i.e. (1) Spirit person; (2) healer; (3) wisdom teacher; and (4) social prophet. Each of these four is learnedly discussed over fourteen illuminating pages, and the fourth clearly shows that, like other social prophets, Jesus' authority "came from the immediacy of [their] experience of God and not from institutional authorization". Yet Borg's attempt to credit Jesus with a further "religious personality", i. e. "(5) movement initiator", I find unconvincing. He sees Jesus' inclusive meal practice as a foreshadowing of the Christian eucharist, which has grown to be deeply exclusive. "His [Jesus'] movement did not move toward institutionalization until quite some time after his death. There was not time for that in his brief life", says Borg, but I submit that there is no evidence that Jesus himself intended "institutionalization" at all. It was his personal ministry, not "his movement", that was "inclusive and egalitarian... [and which] undermined the sharp social boundaries of his day."[2]

Working from the hypothesis of "an alternative view" of how matters progressed after Jesus' death on the cross, I have tried to establish that the official view (enshrined in certain books of Scripture and in the Nicene creed, the Athanasian "creed", and in the liturgy) not only should be challenged, but also has been challenged on many occasions in the past.

But I see my challenge as one with a significant difference. Briefly, it is this: that because God has allowed most of the Christian Church (and here is included not only most of Western Christianity, but the Eastern as well) to teach that Jesus is God Incarnate, as a consequence there have been instituted certain "official" sacraments, with not only their beneficial ends, but also in order to buttress belief in this "all-important" hypothesis. Because these sacraments and their "proper use" for many centuries have formed the basis for the practice of Christian institutional religion, I believe that close examination will reveal not only their own obsolescence, but also that of any institution which continues to teach their necessity and to administer them.

Now, if one will accept that there can be an alternative view of Jesus (i.e. of his nature) then there can be also a different view of the sacraments. In Chapter Six the "theology of sacraments" was set out, as expressed in Cross, for the Seven that were eventually adopted by the Church as "official". Their rationale was based on the Incarnation of God in Jesus, i.e. they were seen as various expressions of the said Incarnation.

The Seven Sacraments used by most of the Christian Church were originally designed to accomplish two things: (i) to reinforce the official teaching that Jesus was both fully human and also fully God (the doctrine of the Incarnation, as set out in the Nicene and other creeds) and (ii) to ensure preservation of the authority of the Church hierarchy, both in teaching and in practice. In some instances, the first reason was paramount, in others it was the second; this is of less consequence than the fact that all but one of them require (under normal circumstances) to be mediated through this hierarchy.

The primary group, of three, was composed of those dealing with the composition of the visible Church, two others were related to the most important aspects of Jesus' earthly ministry, albeit in profoundly misguided ways, another one turned something designed to be a joyful celebration into the most divisive sacrament of all, and finally, one was included in the official list merely to make up the "sacred" number of seven. This last is, of course, marriage, concerning which it has been eventually admitted that the persons marrying each other are the true ministers, the cleric merely conferring a blessing. There are still last-ditch attempts by part of the Church to inject hierarchical "authority" into marriage, for example by refusing admission to the Eucharist to persons marrying "outside the church", but to all intents and purposes, clergy are finally coming to realize that marriage is a joint venture, in respect to which those who marry, whether they believe in God or not, are entitled, mutually, to seek to achieve whatever degree of permanency they consider to be right for them. When a life-long commitment is made, it is capable of being sustained in love only by both persons trusting in their own innate Spirit to strengthen them at times of doubt and stress. If only one of the couple trusts in the Spirit within, a marriage may continue but it will lack (at that point) the joy which arises from mutual love nourished in each by the same Spirit.

Let us now, therefore, consider the other six sacraments, no longer requiring them to illustrate a doctrine of the mythical Incarnation. Three become obsolete and the other three become available to all humanity, as Jesus intended, in non-sacramental form.

The first group deals with membership in the visible Church. First came Baptism, at Pentecost, previously a sign of repentance as taught by John Baptist but then expanded to include the "giving of the Spirit" through the use of Jesus' name.[3] Later it became taught that this "giving of the Spirit" came through the laying on of hands by one of the apostles or their accredited successors. As whole families, including children, became baptized, and as the Church communities spread, the membership ritual divided into two parts, that of Baptism itself, saving from damnation and conferring "membership" even upon infants, and that of Confirmation, which involved the individual making promises regarding the nature of belief and the laying on of (usually) episcopal hands to guarantee the "reception" of the Spirit. These were the two sacraments, then, for "full membership"; a third was for the hierarchy: Holy Orders was its name, designed to ensure that orthodoxy was maintained and taught by a select few, set apart by those already selected. These Holy Orders became three-layered, with the top-most known as bishops, all of whom had been raised to their eminence through the laying on of hands by other bishops, right back through the centuries, to those who had received the laying on of hands, it is claimed, from the original apostles themselves. This guarantee of apostolic lineage became known as "apostolic succession"; the Church was thus not only visible, but it was physically linked to those who had known Jesus upon earth. For some reason, this was declared to be essential. Yet, as we have seen, it did not prevent sections of this visible body from declaring other sections to be "excommunicated" as "heretics".

There is no better illustration of how the use of sacraments delimited and so emasculated the prime elements of Jesus' teaching than the group of two designed for healing and for reconciliation. These two are so inter-related that, in a way, they truly are "one", as shown in the wonderful account of Jesus' healing of the paralytic man let down through the roof: [4] here is a man who was ill, both physically and also psychologically, in the sense of being burdened with sin, quite possibly in a way that he had kept to himself, perhaps some alienation from his fellow-men through an act against another or an omission which only he knew to have been wrong. Jesus' healed both his physical injury and also his psychological ill, or sin, utilizing both the outward and visible faith of those who brought him and the personal, inward desire of the man himself for forgiveness, despite there being no record of this latter being articulated or made known to Jesus in any way, other than that they would have doubtless made eye-contact. This two-fold action is what always occurs in healing of this nature, with the physical or visible side being observed by others with amazement and the psychological or invisible side being received with thankfulness by the sufferer. The outward showing of this gratitude is well illustrated by the single one of the ten lepers returning to Jesus to give thanks even though ten were physically cleansed.[5] He recognized the reality of his inner cleansing while the other nine apparently were content with the physical alone and were thus only partially healed.

So it is in the world today: to be healed physically without realizing the wonderful opportunity to begin a life newly at peace in one's relationships with others is to be healed incompletely. It was this complete healing that Jesus meant to be made available to others. He sent those who followed him out to accomplish this. When they failed, he told them that it was due specifically to their failure to persevere in prayer.[6] There are records of healings throughout Acts, performed by Peter and John, but by the time the epistle of James came to be written, most likely in the 80s or 90s, it had become a stylized effort of calling for the elders to pray and to lay hands upon the afflicted person.[7] This is not to disparage the "touching" of an ill person, which often, but not always, was Jesus' way, but to note that the power to carry this out was already being seen to be the province of the "elders", that is, those who had been admitted to Holy Orders, rather than of all who believed. Eventually both of these liberating actions of Jesus (healing and forgiveness) became corrupted into "Extreme Unction" and "Penance", relying upon the presence of clergy for their validity.[8] Lay individuals (i.e. those not in Holy Orders) claiming to have, through prayer and counselling, the ability to heal and to lift the burden of sin from others, have always been suspect in the visible Church. The Oxford Dictionary of the Christian Church contains entries for both "Penance" and "Unction", but for neither "Forgiveness" nor "Healing", which is a good indication of how, at least until the twentieth century, these two aspects of Jesus' historical ministry had been stylized into "Sacraments".

Penance – the name itself comes from "*poena*" – meaning "punishment" – was so strict in the early Church, being permitted only once in one's lifetime, that confession of sin was usually delayed until death approached, and similarly, because Unction became so bound up with Penance, it too was similarly delayed until the sufferer was "*in extremis*", hence the title "Extreme Unction". Later, more than one fall from grace was allowed but yet, the penitent having confessed his sin, the practice was to delay forgiveness, called Absolution, until the penance had been completed. Later still, Absolution was given after Confession, and a lighter Penance given. For unworthy reasons, this sacrament developed many complications, such as commutation, the issuing of indulgences, and the Treasury of Merit, all devised by the medieval church and far from Jesus' intention. "At every stage, the ability of the Church to intercede for sinners and the power of its ministers to absolve and reconcile them has lain behind the theology of Penance."[9] Unction has been so linked with Penance over centuries that its healing potential has gone unremarked until the twentieth. Today our understanding of the ubiquitous power of the "healing touch" means that no longer is there any limitation to the use of one specific method, such as Unction, nor to any specific "kind" of person, such as one in Holy Orders. Finally mankind is beginning to perceive that both healing and forgiveness are aspects of a "holistic" view of human nature, and that it is through personal relationships that they are achieved. Scientific research, medical and nursing skill, and trained counsellors all are important for healing and reconciliation, including the personal dedication of each professional who is involved; the additional key factor is the trust of the person or persons concerned that there is a purpose in the whole process, and that the purpose is "good". It is the function, or opportunity, of those who are in a personal relationship with those concerned, to nurture this trust in "a good purpose" through close support in any number of ways, always including prayer or its equivalent.[10] Empathy is a new word to express this new understanding of how we are all important to others, through our relationships. Thus the sacraments of Penance and Unction, administered under the authority of those in Holy Orders, have no place in implementing the twin actions of healing and reconciliation, which always includes forgiveness. Jesus demonstrated this many times in his earthly ministry; many others, whether acquainted with Jesus' works or not, have done the same – the opportunity is always available for all who choose to seize it.

And so we come to the final "official" sacrament, known as the Holy Communion, Mass, Lord's Supper, and Eucharist. This sacrament has been the cause of argument and division over many centuries, sprouting whole libraries of learned volumes and innumerable variations of doctrine, ranging from the "Real Presence" to the "Real Absence" [of Jesus] in the elements.[11] All this has ensured both superstition and confusion among Jesus' followers, both those inside and those said to be outside the visible church.

What was far from Jesus' intention was that his words should have been so interpreted as to form a completely new commandment, one which would, against early hopes of providing unity, continue to divide his followers for two thousand years, beginning as early as the first century. It is likely that Peter saw, at Pentecost, how helpful enjoying a meal together would be for the "new fellowship", whether at this point it resembled *agapé* (a feast of love), or a remembrance of the apostles' final supper with Jesus. But when the first communities became aware of God's spirit within them, and broke bread together, as Jesus had, not only (be it remembered) with his followers but also with tax collectors and sinners, it was Paul who in his fevered imagination decided otherwise. He decided that this genuine way of expressing a loving acceptance of all present (modelled on the principle of Jesus' many 'inclusive' meals), spontaneous, joyful and unbounded by any rules, ought to be changed into a repetitive, controlled, magical (later refined to "sacramental") re-appearance of Jesus "hidden" in the basic elements of food and drink. His first indication of this appears in a passage that is not a question but a rhetorical statement:

> *Is not the cup of thanksgiving for which we give thanks a participation in the blood of Christ? And is not the bread that we break a participation in the body of Christ?*[12]

It is how he builds upon this that has so influenced those who have read this letter, accepting it as a rhetorical truth. In the following chapter Paul pursues his theme by daring to state:

For I received from the Lord what I also passed on to you: The Lord Jesus, on the night he was betrayed, took bread, and when he had given thanks, he broke it and said, 'This is my body, which is for you; do this in remembrance of me'. In the same way, after supper he took the cup, saying, 'This cup is the new covenant in my blood; do this, whenever you drink it, in remembrance of me'.[13]

The first and most important point is that Paul had no direct contact with Jesus during the latter's lifetime. Only from the Damascus road "voice" from heaven[14] and from his actual "appearance", (presumably at the same time)[15] is Jesus made known to Paul; but now we are told that Jesus also communicated to Paul details of events at the supper with his disciples, including specific words spoken at that time. Did this also happen at the same time as when he was thrown to the ground and blinded? It is more probable that Paul's imagination took over: his rhetorical statement (above) leading him to see a way to promote unity through universal participation in a ritual meal, and his pharisaical inclinations urging him to insist that only the pure should participate in this ritual.[16]

Once the other leaders (possibly abetted by the priests newly-converted) saw how their control could be extended from a ceremony of admitting to membership to one that included all such gatherings of believers, the meal became a sacrament, with table transformed into altar and Jesus' ministry entirely focussed upon his death.[17] Paul's rhetorical style combined with sacrificial metaphor has thus let loose the imaginations of generations of theologians to extend, to refine and to dispute.[18] And so Luke, Paul's companion, added to Jesus' statement, "*This is my body*" (found in all three synoptic gospels)[19] the words of Paul's "great idea", namely, "*[which is] given for you. Do this in remembrance of me,*"[20] words which had been written in the epistle (see above) well before Luke's gospel had come into existence. This addition, of course, was to ensure belief that this sacrament had been actually authorized by Jesus himself.

The second of Luke's intrusions is also important: when Jesus gave the cup to his disciples, according to the earliest versions of Matthew and Mark, he used the phrase "*my blood of the covenant*" while only Luke has the word "*new*", inserted before "*covenant*", which also comes from Paul's stated recollection of Jesus' words.[21] For Paul, Jesus had to be introducing a new covenant, yet one still tied to membership and ritual, as a Pharisee would expect.

Must this view of mine therefore make the "Last Supper", which in Christianity has evolved into the Sacrament of the Eucharist, meaningless? Definitely not. I recently discovered a book entitled *Rabbi Jesus: An Intimate Biography*.[22] In it the author is persuaded that it meant a great deal to Jesus. His is indeed a well-researched book, in which his view that Jesus was a prophetic rabbi in the tradition of Elijah and Elisha is carefully advanced throughout. This is not the place to summarize the book, nor am I competent to do so, but the author did come to an important conclusion about Jesus' intention to give a new meaning to the Judaistic temple offering, which I believe has relevance to my view.

I understand that Professor Chilton maintains Jesus' teaching to have been that the true sacrifice of Israel's people to God was not the blood and flesh of animals offered by the temple priests upon their altar. Rather, it was the people's offering of themselves that was the true offering, whereas that of the animals merely symbolized it. Throughout his prophetic ministry Jesus used meal-gatherings as opportunities for him to evidence this: people were able to offer themselves directly to God through this friendly and inclusive socialization; no priests or levites were required for mediatorial roles, nor was a sacred place needed. Jesus taught that this pleased God: it was to be seen as God's way for the Kingdom of Heaven to be "brought to earth".[23]

This tallies with my thesis that when people gather together it is their ability and also their privilege to "lift up their hearts" in thanksgiving for having been created "human". Take the "*Sursum Corda*" – the usual translation is "Lift up your hearts!" – spoken in the service of Holy Communion by the bishop or priest with the response from the congregation "We lift them to the Lord!". These twin shouts of joy are to me the high point of the entire service.[24] They occur just prior to what the Church considers the most solemn and important part (the offering of the bread and wine by means of the Prayer of Consecration), yet surely the lifting to God of one's own heart, a figurative expression of offering one's whole being, including the spirit, is of greater value than whatever material items have been placed upon the altar. Such offering pleases God, in any social context whatever, even when there may be no acknowledgement of how those who are expressing recognition of their Good Spirit consider whence it came: it is enough that they possess it and intend to use it for good. This is their offering; no longer need there be sacraments involving mediators between the whole people of God and their Creator.

At times there have been well-meant attempts to justify this "Lord's Supper" sacrament as a means toward Christian unity. But argument and division do not lessen as more ecumenical and inclusive views are advanced; it seems rather to be the principal "stumbling-stone" of all attempts to promote peace and harmony among Christian believers. This is because such attempts are institutionally organized, and therefore ecclesiastically-centred. "That they may all be one" means, ecclesiastically, a single institution, powerful and visible, dominated by whichever of the presently divided sections prevails. This is neither possible nor desirable; indeed, "statements of organizational unity" had never formed any part of Jesus' intention.

On the theme of unity, this is what Jesus taught: that human beings should live in a "family fellowship" with one another, accepting all differences, racial, cultural, economic and social, as being completely irrelevant to such amity.[25] Nowhere in his earthly ministry [apart from the single intrusion of Peter's "commission"] does he advocate formation of a new institution. Everyone has to eat; food is essential to human existence; and Jesus' words at the final meal with his followers need have meant no more than that he was, emphatically and decisively, completely human, with absolutely no hint of a "special" divine nature. That portion of God's nature that inhabited him, known as God's spirit, also inhabits each and every member of humankind. The task bequeathed to his followers, and to all, was to display this spirit in such manner that all who came in contact with them in turn became aware of that same spirit within themselves, and so were able to show it forth to others. True, his blood was to be poured out for many, in the sense that he was prepared to give his entire life for others right up to death: he knew this, even as all to whom he passed the cup that night were also intended to have their life blood used up in such service. No longer were humans (as in more primitive times) nor even animals to be used as "sacrificial offerings" to placate a jealous God. He taught that God was a loving father, a creator who desired only that human beings would come to realize that they were all children of a single family, and as such would be prepared "to love all others as themselves". This of course included renunciation of violence, demonstrated fully by Jesus' acceptance of the manner of his death. He was able to offer his entire life, not merely his death, because of his reliance upon God's will, made known to him day by day through their steadfast communion, night by night, in prayer.

It is my conviction that the straightforward words common to all three gospels indicate that Jesus meant his whole adult life to be seen as the culmination of the original covenant, from his baptism by John to his death on the cross. Then, indeed, there would be a new covenant, but one as prophesied by Jeremiah:[26] a true coming of God's kingdom upon earth, but one unfettered by need of any institutional membership or ritual.

Notes - Chapter 9 – The Obsolete Seven

1. Hick 1977 (for complete book references see Bibliography) Hick has edited ten important essays, all of which conclude, from various viewpoints, this credal belief [that Jesus is God Incarnate] to be an error.

2. Borg & Wright 2000, pp. 60-74.

3. (John Baptist's view of Jesus' ministry) It is useful at this point to note how the gospel accounts vary. Mark reads "he (Jesus) will baptize you with the Holy Spirit" (Mk 1:8) but both Matt. and Luke have him adding "with fire" and continuing with a winnowing-fork metaphor. (Mt 3:11-12; Lk 3:16-17). That was very much Peter's view (Acts 2:40), that is, it was to separate people (wheat from chaff) in readiness for the fire of God's judgement, and thus a continuation of John's kind of baptism ("Who warned you to flee from the wrath to come?" (Mt 3:7; Lk 3:7). Only Mark's account understands Jesus' primary ministry not to be that of judgement between wheat and chaff, but of offering healing and reconciliation for all.

4. (Jesus Heals A paralytic) Mk 2:1-12; Mt 9:1-8; Lk 5:17-26

5. (Ten Healed of Leprosy) Lk 17:11-19.

6. (What the Disciples Lacked) Mk 9:29. Two of the earliest manuscripts (the 'middle fourth century' Codex Sinaiticus, "S", and the 'fourth century' Codex Vaticanus, "B", see Throckmorton 1992, pp. xiv, xv) have "through prayer" only (Throckmorton 1992, p. 104, footnote "L"); later ones add "and fasting", an attempt to add an outward observance not contemplated by Jesus.

7. (Duty of the Sick Person) James 5:14-15. However, the closing verses (5:16-end) show that, in those very early days, confession of sins "to each other" (obviously including reciprocal forgiveness) antedated the establishment of the sacrament of Penance.

8. (A Crippled Beggar is Healed) (Acts 3:1-10) The prominence given Peter and John in their healings by Luke, and the claim, in only one gospel (Mt 16:19), that Jesus had both founded a church upon one of his followers and given that same person the power both to forgive and to withhold forgiveness, is evidence of how greatly both Luke and the compiler of "the gospel of Matthew" must have relied upon accounts given by Peter and John themselves, or by their loyal followers. From this beginning, both healing and forgiveness would later be declared to be sacramental, and thus the exclusive prerogative of those in Holy Orders.

9. ODCC 1977, p. 1250.

10. It is impossible, indeed churlish, to deny that the sincere and heart-felt statements of concerns for others (e.g. "I shall be thinking of you", "I am sending you 'good vibes'.") made by persons at a stage in their lives when they do not acknowledge God's existence may be just as efficacious as the prayers of believers. See my final chapter.

11. I have no evidence (having not sought it) that the doctrine of the "Real Absence" of Jesus in the elements of this sacrament was actually taught in Anglican seminaries although it doubtless occurred in some segments of Christianity. The phrase, in jocular use when I was a theological student, was due to the words above a painting over the chapel altar of the seminary across the road ("he [Jesus] is risen; he is not here", Mk 16:6, King James version). As the celebrant read the Prayer of Consecration, it was possible to imagine that the figures in the painting were indicating the elements before him rather than the grave. Such jejune humour is now thankfully gone in Canada, I believe. Yet I am told that in England there remains even today an Anglican seminary permitted to train future clergy committed to denying the validity of their priestly orders when held by women of their own Communion. Ought one to laugh or weep? Surely it must be both.

12. (Paul's Idea) I Cor. 10:16.

13. (Paul's Idea Developed) I Cor. 11:23-25.

14. (What Saul [later, Paul] Heard) Acts 9:3-5; 22:6-8; 26:13-15.

15. (Paul's Vision of the Risen Jesus) I Cor. 15:8. There are divergent opinions about whether a light and a voice came to Paul [Saul] (Luke's version in Acts, note 14 above) or an actual appearance of the risen Jesus (as Paul says here). Brown 1997, pp. 534-5.

16. (Paul 'Knows' How 'the Lord' Judges 'Unworthy' Communicants) I Cor. 11:27-34.

17. (How Paul's Idea is to be Proclaimed) I Cor. 11:26.

18. Brown 1997, p. 538 (Issue 8).

19. (The Institution of the Lord's Supper) (Mt 26:26; Mk 14:22; Lk 22:19).

20. (One Gospel puts Paul's Idea into Jesus' Words) (Lk 22:19b only).

21. (Paul's Idea expressed as a New Covenant) (Mt 26:28; Mk 14:24; Lk 22:20). The word "*new*" appears in neither Matt. nor Mark in two of the earliest sources (manuscripts "S" and "B", Throckmorton 1992, p. 184, footnotes "Y" and "Z"; see also note 6 above). In later sources, however, it does appear.

22. Chilton 2002. For the complete reference for this book, see Bibliography.

23. Chilton 2002, pp. 250-7. I have not done justice to the author's full insights.

24. "*Sursum Corda*" – Indeed, these two words form a command with the imperative verb understood: "Hearts, On High!" and similar words are used by us in many different contexts, which is the way it ought to be. I think especially of my days at sea in the Navy when sharp at noon came the welcome pipe: "Up, spirits!" For most of us aboard, was there ever a more cheerful "*double-entendre*"?

25. "The other great religious insight illuminated by the Human Genome Project is the unity of the human family. Genetically, we are one species: there is no scientific basis whatever for notions of racial superiority or inferiority. What a piece of work is a man! ... and the design is awesome." *Reading the Creator's Code*, leading editorial, The Tablet, July 1, 2000, p. 883.

26. (The New Covenant, still awaited in its fullness) Jer. 31:31-34.

Recognizing The Spirit Within Us

Part III – The Future: Recognition
The Spirit is Within Us All

Chapter 10: Freeing The Spirit:
For Both Believer and Non-Believer

Here I have repeated the *Note of concern* because my book, most specifically in this chapter, is addressed not only to those who believe in God's existence but also to those who hold atheistic and agnostic positions.

This is because I wish to emphasize a fundamental error of many religions up to now: that humanity has "fallen" – from grace and into sin – and that the gods who wield supernatural power must be propitiated in ways "known to" certain persons, who teach

(Note of concern: as this book claims to be of value to both believer and non-believer, I trust readers considering themselves to be of the latter category will understand my difficulty in avoiding mention of God. May I ask that you kindly substitute any word that conveys your understanding that a Spirit of, or Desire for, Goodness does exist in each person, its origin undeclared)

those "who do not know" how to obey the "instructions from above". Anthropologists have shown how societies world-wide reacted to adverse events deemed "supernatural", i.e. caused by "the gods". They relied upon a person, or persons, who could tell the rest of them "what to do" in order to find favour once again with the gods, and so they obeyed.

Even in the Judeo-Christian and Islamic traditions, when "the gods" had been replaced by "God", this idea continued. Humanity had displeased God, right from the beginning, and the only way for people to overcome this displeasure was to obey certain persons claiming to "know" what God wanted and who were thus responsible for relaying these "Godly instructions". Leaders had moved from witch-doctor and "wise man" to rabbi, minister and imam, but the same principle remained in place. Let temporal authority be the province of chieftains, emperors, generals or presidents, supernatural authority was always to be granted to the spiritual leaders – those who knew what God desired. And the leaders had to be obeyed because human beings always started off as "Fallen", i.e."guilty of offending God". Indeed, to some leaders, this was by identifying "carnally born", i.e. the usual manner of birth, as being "born in sin", hence the phrase "Original Sin". The stories of the development of the closely-linked theories of The Fall [of Mankind, see Genesis Ch. 2,3] and of Original Sin [of Humanity] are amazing when read today.[1] From them it appears that instead of recognizing the very powerful "animal" instincts still present in us all, Christian apologists continue to insist that giving play to these instincts is exclusively a moral choice; therefore yielding to them is always "sinning". The increasing weight of evidence, primarily through studies in history, psychology and sociology, reveals that humanity is very gradually overcoming the selfish aspect of such instincts; but this is disregarded by the religious institutions; Paul's "idea" that the death of one man "redeemed the sins of the world" has been inculcated into so many persons over two millennia that many still take it to be literally true.

However, the message, sometimes coded, sometimes explicit, through observation of Jesus' life and from attending to his teaching, is that God's will is to be done by mankind through person-to-person relationships, both individual and group, and not through following the rules of any institution specifically based on the existence of God. This is of course not to deny the existence of many relationships between members of such institutions that issue in furtherance of God's will: I seek merely to maintain that their validity does not depend upon membership but upon each person's Spirit within.

The whole tenor of Jesus' life shows this: he took what is good from the Old Testament Scriptures; he meditated upon it; he asked questions of his elders; he prayed for guidance. Surviving his temptations, which were not neatly packaged as an "examination" to be "passed" but doubtless plagued him all his life, he "lived a life" of seeking to do God's will, showing it forth as it seemed right to him. Jesus refused to claim any external authority. The case can be made that "he spoke and acted *without authority* and that he regarded "the exercise of authority" as a pagan characteristic."[2]

"The English word 'authority' is usually reserved for the right to be obeyed by people.... Nothing could be more unauthoritative than the parables of Jesus. Their whole purpose is to enable listeners to discover something for themselves."[3] They are of two main kinds: those spoken in response to questions from his opponents are designed to end with a question also (explicit or implicit) seeking to persuade them.[4] Those of the other kind, sayings as well as parables, may be perceived as authoritative but do not rely upon any outside authority, neither rabbinical tradition nor even scripture itself.[5] That is why the people were so amazed. Indeed when challenged to declare the source of his authority, he refused to answer.[6] "Jesus was unique among the people of his time in his ability to overcome all forms of authority-thinking."[7] This was because he was offering "an alternative wisdom... the primary purpose [being] to invite hearers into a different way of seeing – of seeing God, themselves, and life itself."[8] Jesus' awareness of the reality of God rested entirely within himself, and he relied upon this interior experience, accepting ultimately that such experience could be trusted right to the moment of death, but never proved.[9]

And so, in future discussions about the relation of humanity to God, the concept of "trust" needs to displace that of "faith". The latter word has become so heavily encrusted with man's doctrinal assertions about God's nature, that its primary meaning of "faithfulness" has been greatly obscured.

This, then, is the pattern, the formula, for every person's life: to accept what the day offers for reconciliation, for healing, for serving others, in whatever ways open up. Jesus took each day as it came, living and teaching "with authority", but it was an authority derived solely from God's presence within himself. There is nothing new about this; God's presence within all humanity is a recurring theme of the mystics as well as of many writers today. "God is already united to us. He is united to us all the time; it is only our awareness of this union that increases. For this is precisely the difference between God and the created beings of the world: God is within. 'God is more interior to us than we are ourselves'."[10]

No institution is needed to provide "authority". No sacraments are required to mediate strength of spirit, called "grace". We have both within us. This becomes apparent from study of the record of Jesus' life and teaching. For having this record we must be grateful to those who have ensured that the genuine wheat of Jesus' life and teachings has been preserved, even though buried within the chaff that has accumulated over so many centuries.

The revelation of God's true nature and intention has come through to humanity only very gradually. We have seen how, in Jesus' personal ministry, God's goodness, and love for all persons, were unfolded to us. As he encountered different people, he began to realize more deeply the extent of God's love and the innateness of God's goodness in all humanity. As he ministered, more and more did he realize that all people needed to make this discovery for themselves: hence the universality of his parables.

As this new concept of the Good Spirit's presence within each person was taught by Jesus, the need for external authority imposed by a hierarchy of "those specially chosen to rule" and to mediate God's spiritual "grace" (or power) through keeping "religious observances" (later called, by the Church, sacraments) was to fade out of existence. The fact that it did not do so was due to either Jesus' followers' failure to comprehend his message or their unwillingness to accept it. The notion of spiritual authority as something working outward from within each person was just too radical – too far-fetched – to be believed. And so occurred the events of "The Past" set out in my first six chapters.

It is now clear that a key aspect of both Jesus' life and teaching was the primacy and sufficiency of personal prayer. However, the word "prayer", like that of "faith", has become so overladen by meanings placed upon it by various persons over the centuries that its basic meaning has been obscured. All agree that it concerns our relationship to God, which can also be seen as how we connect with our Good Spirit within. Through looking at the record of how Jesus prayed, for me three words come to mind.

The first is *Union*. Because God is in each of us in Spirit, Jesus knew his praying was an internal matter. This is not to deny that God, as Creator of all, is also "out there" but to recognize that the interior aspect is the one for fruitful union. The technical term for this is "panentheism", which, unlike "pantheism", holds both aspects of God, i.e. both the reality of God's Spirit within human beings and also the reality of the Wholly Other, the Creator, to be true.[11] Jesus' mind communed with this Spirit daily, each night and morning and also at moments of decision as they arose. It was this that gave him his insight for action, called "an intuitive and self-authenticating experience."[12]

The second word is *Attention.* The human mind is so arranged as to be able to hold together multiple thoughts, all seeking for attention at any given moment. This is what makes achieving awareness of this ability for mind and Spirit to be united in oneself so difficult. There are multitudes of books to assist us in concentrating upon God's presence as we pray, some helpful for some, others for others, but I have found the best method for "Attention" is a plain acknowledgement of two things: God's presence within me, and my need for insight, both expressed in a deep awareness of their connectedness.

The third word is *Action.* This refers both to God's action within us and also to one's own. There is no way that anyone can presume to separate these two, and this is not really a dilemma, merely a witness to what has been expressed thus: "[God's] acting in us is nearer and more inward than our own actions. God works in us from inside outwards; creatures work on us from the outside."[13] When Jesus says "Be compassionate as God is compassionate"[14] he is showing us "*A new way of living...* The core value of Jesus' ethic was compassion... seeing people not with cultural categories, important or unimportant, deserving or undeserving, but as beloved of God.... Thus a far more inclusive social vision was possible."[15] And the reason it "was possible" is because God's Spirit, called by some "The Spirit of Goodness", in a mysterious way, is within each person.

From the above it can reasonably be held that all mankind has received, ever since it began as a species, a certain portion / component / virtue / attribute, the proper word is of no importance: it is *something* of God's nature. On an intellectual level, its origin need not be ascribed to God: it is just there, within us. This *something* could be termed compassion / love for others / even, simply, goodness; it is *something* that has been given to each of us, if we will but recognize it. To describe just how one senses that this forms part of the nature of every human being is difficult: it is truly an "awareness": of a sense of right and wrong (conscience); of a sense of purpose beyond one's own earthly survival; of a sense of the possibility of reality beyond the world, the universe, indeed beyond all "matter". This "awareness" is a mystery, but not an illusion, not a myth. Moreover, it is when this *something* in human nature (called by many, "Spirit") is joined to humanity's evolved self-consciousness and still-evolving free-will, that good actions issue forth in our lives.

Ways of expressing this are many, and they are all positive:

1) People learn from one another, through direct contact with others; through hearing about others' words and deeds; through reading accounts of such words and deeds.

2) People also learn through their own inner experiences, and endeavour to communicate such experiences to others.

3) People tend to act in accordance with instinct, received from evolution, but, under certain conditions, may choose rather to act in accordance with this other part of their nature, which is always present within them, but which requires both effort and intention, or purpose, to be activated.

4) The intention is to "do right" / to "seek the good".

5) The intention must be considered by the person to be worth the effort.

6) The reason why this intention is considered worth the effort is because the persons concerned trust that there is purpose in both their own life-decisions and also in the way such decisions impact upon the total world situation.

From the foregoing, I have devised an acronym, admittedly clumsy but which I have found helpful in expressing the point: **ASIA**, standing for *Awareness of Shared Interior Authority*. One's authority arises only from the alignment of one's own will with that of God's Spirit, which alignment is discovered through steadfast prayer. The obvious problem here for the believer is to keep one's self-will from always prevailing, in the often self-deceptive guise of claiming that it is "supported by God's Spirit within me". Similarly, a person unconvinced of the reality of God might express it thus: "My authority arises from the alignment of my own will with my desire to do the right thing", the pitfall here being "my desire is always right!") There are thus ever-present dangers for both believers and non-believers, and there can be no single way guaranteed to guard against it. Yet ways must be found. One such way, advocated by the Society of Friends, is through the submission of an individual's "idea for action" to the patient scrutiny and prayerful response of others, in order that any one person's "Interior Authority" or concept of "the right thing" may be tested through being shared. This is of particular importance when the proposed "idea for action" is of social significance. Thus, "to obtain a sense of the meeting" is a wise way to test such ideas, and I have obtained permission to reproduce, towards the end of this chapter, "*Foundations of a true social order*", which were the result of three years' prayerful deliberation by Friends in the early twentieth century.

This new way of evaluating one's life-decisions ought not to be motivated by whether or not they will bring one to eternal life, but by whether they advance humanity's development in this world, either in the present time or in the future. The greater part of humanitarian writing today may or may not be cast in the "religious" form of "bringing in the Kingdom of God" or "doing God's will", because writers now recognize that progress depends upon as many persons as possible seeking to "do the right thing", regardless of their intellectual attitude to the existence of a Creator God. Putting it into as succinct a form as possible, the correct attitude for all thinking persons, in their relationships with others so concerned is no longer "I'm O.K.; you will be, too, if you believe as I do". Rather, it is (as I recall from a book-title) "*I'm O.K.,You're O.K.*."[16]

This non-judgmental attitude to others was the secret of Jesus' own ministry, and has been the quiet way for both believers in God and unbelievers to proceed upon this path of developing humanity's nature. We have come far enough upon this path for us now to realize that segregation of any kind militates against further progress; protestations of "I believe in God" and of "There is no God" alike mean nothing unless those who make them work together for good in the present time. It should be emphasized that protestations of the attainment of eternal life for those who "believe in God in the proper fashion" must now be seen as matters not of certainty, but of trust, as it was for Jesus upon the Cross. Even if, in the 2,000 years of the history of the Christian Church, belief in attainment of eternal life was taught as being the primary motivation for persons to "do what is right", it should be seen today as limited and essentially self-centred, properly repelling thinking persons as being a "carrot-inspired" reason for obeying the Church's rules and articulating the Church's credal statements as facts.

The reason why the "pull" to believe in eternal life has been so strong, and therefore has, up to now, worked so well, is because it is a residual of the earthly-survival instinct which has evolved from all earlier forms of life. Wittingly or not at first, the Church has seized on this as a powerful way to control its members. It transmogrified simple, prayerful trust in God as exemplified in Jesus' earthly ministry into a belief-system centred upon exaggerating his person to God-status and identifying the meaning of his obedient death as the redemption of all humanity. Much of this, as we have seen, came about largely through the good intentions of one prominent Pharisee to "win over" others, by letters and preaching, to his personal view. A few simple fishermen had preceded him and many devout intellectuals have followed him. Human beings, assisted by the faculty of self-consciousness, have always been tempted to achieve power through the domination of their own ideas over those of others. But God foresaw this, and has revealed the Divine Intention, as well as the Divine Nature, only gradually, over many centuries and through many persons, both believers and doubters.

So then, this opens up the way forward for all thinking people. The truth about God is one of two propositions: God exists; or God does not exist. Each person's response to this will vary in intensity and confidence depending upon both interior and exterior factors of daily life, ranging from complete intellectual certainty that "God is", through the spectrum of doubt (God may/may not exist), to complete intellectual certainty that "God is not". The principal point here is that, whatever may be one's "view" at any particular point of time, the uniquely human attribute mentioned above and known under so many names, one of which is "Inner Light",[17] has been imbedded from birth in every person, and therefore that the intellectual answer itself is not of first importance; what really matters is "the life lived" by each and every person, day by day.

The temptation has always been not merely to hold that one or other of the above propositions is true, which is self-evident, but to claim to know which is the true one. Indeed, one of the most prominent of the many respected individuals claiming to know that "There is no God" very cleverly urges us to take advantage of all the good that has come about through believing that "God is" and then to transmute all this into a belief that it was evolution's path to "full humanity". He holds that this evolutionary process began through instillation of a belief in the existence of "God", gradually refined over centuries to include all the virtues, and destined to emerge fully-fledged in humans, with only one more thing to be done. If I understand him correctly, this would be to accept that the keeping of the virtues would be achieved more successfully by everyone acting "as if there were a God" urging them to be moral and benevolent, while acknowledging at the same time that "belief in God" is in reality belief in a myth, an evolutionary arrangement for the ultimate emergence of "moral mankind".

> "We have conducted a long campaign against theological realism and in the course of it have taken leave of the God of metaphysical theism. We have sought to describe instead a modern and fully-autonomous spirituality ... God is a myth we have to have ... We have to go forward

to a new kind of faith which is fully conscious. It uses myth, but it also transcends it into autonomy."[18]

For believer or non-believer in God, to choose one hypothesis or the other, and then to proclaim that one's own choice must be the right one, such insistence leading to endless verbal debate and with no decision possible: is this to be the only way forward? Is this the way chosen by God? The God who has compassion upon all? I believe not.

Rather, I believe that the viewpoint holding that human beings ought to act "as if" God exists is not necessarily displeasing to God. Nor, indeed, is the third possible position, called agnosticism, that because it is impossible to know whether God exists or not, one should remain ambivalent, refusing to take one side or the other. There are many persons today using gifts of healing and reconciliation in the course of their selfless service of others, some who deny God's existence intellectually, others who refuse to attempt either to affirm or to deny God's existence. Such lives of service would tally, in their relationships with others, with that of Jesus' own life and ministry. Indeed, Jesus' whole life is one of autonomous decisions, yet taken secure in the awareness that God's Spirit was within him, and this would continue to be the example for both believers and unbelievers, even though the latter would not so describe their humanitarian inner impulse. He knew that he could not "prove" his trust in his heavenly Father's existence; he could only live it. He did not order us to believe; he left the record of his life.

My conclusion is that the intellectual position adopted by any person: be it theistic, atheistic or agnostic, truly does not matter to God so much as the way each person lives. If all persons are willing to work together, some praying and acting, some meditating and acting, others content to concentrate always upon the task at hand as they act, then this would result in world harmony through mutual concern in all neighbourly matters. The true humanitarian description of this word, "neighbours", would be seen, in all its many positive ranges of meaning, for example, family, local community and global scope, to have the same meaning as that intended by God.[19] Humankind would attempt to exclude no person from the respect due to every human being, which would lead, very gradually to our impatient minds, probably over centuries, to the refusal to see as barriers all differences of race, language, national borders and gender. Also to be discarded would be statements of belief which any particular institution claims are "completely true" about God; nothing in words of man can encompass God's wholeness.

This leads to a further conclusion that, while group acknowledgement of God's existence has been regarded, in the past, as a pre-requisite for "bringing in God's kingdom upon earth", or "doing God's will", we can now move to the position that each person's endeavour to implement that which is both "right" and possible, is more important than such acknowledgement. Many who do believe in God are now, in this third millennium, coming to see that their resulting trust in that existence is to be based upon a new understanding of the divine nature, i.e. that God is to be seen as no longer jealous, no longer vengeful, and no longer holding out the prospect of "Paradise" as a "special incentive" to themselves, but rather as content to exercise infinite loving patience while encouraging all humanity to travel its long road to peaceful coexistence. Consequently, this trust is to move them to live in harmony and mutual respect with all other persons, completely willing to share with them the desire to advance the cause of universal compassion throughout the world.

By relinquishing the claim that the achievement of eternal life is one's principal "engine" for belief, this claim being located most forcefully in the context of membership in religious institutions, then the attempt to live one's own life for the benefit of others can be given its proper place. The temptation to membership in any organization which uses evangelistic, and therefore ultimately dominative, power can thus be resisted, permitting the interior gifts of meekness, patience, and compassion for others possessed by all persons to be exercised mutually, in both the development of individual talents and also through what in the past have been seen as "secular" groupings. Many of these seek to advance the good of all humanity and are therefore truly inclusive, in contrast to some "religious" ones, unfortunately required to be exclusive through their claims.

Throughout all "religious" history, up to the present day, there has been the assertion, both explicitly declared and implicitly felt, that communal worship (under whatever name or form) is the most important action of all in pleasing God. The motives have varied over the centuries, as the true nature of God has been gradually revealed, chronologically and geographically, throughout the world. Such motives have included fear, appeasement, desire for prosperity, relief from disaster, victory over enemies and the attainment of eternal life. They have stemmed from the most elemental awareness of the supernatural, developing into an awakening belief in nature gods, gods of "the earth and sky", pantheons of super-humans, household gods, tribal deities, and, in more than one tradition, have evolved into belief in a single God, who has revealed aspects of the divine nature at variance with earlier understandings. Yet even Jesus', and others', teachings on the need for progress in the development of such "humane" attributes that we all possess have continued to be made subservient to membership in one or other particular "religious" institution, with each committed to proclaiming that the outward worship of God must take priority. But back in the psalmist's time, when animal sacrifice was believed an essential part of human worship ceremonies, God had made known that "every animal of the forest is mine, and the cattle on a thousand hills."[20] The clue was there, that although to be group-worshipped may not be displeasing to God, it is not God's primary concern. And now that fuller awareness of God's nature has come to mankind over the centuries, it is time for us to get on with the commandment that ought to be in front of our eyes each day: *to love our neighbour as ourself.*

This is now appreciated not only by individuals but also by at least one religious organization: that of the Society of Friends, or Quakers. Although "membership" does exist, it seems to be primarily to assist, through mutual support, each member's personal development of awareness of that Inner Light, which is God's Spirit within. The urge to draw new members from other groups, religious or not, is absent; even atheists are re-assured that their intellectual position remains a matter only for themselves[21] – an approach much more God-trusting than the conventional Christian one of "Why not come and worship with us?" which occasionally means "We hope that you will join us." Corporate silence, which is the essential part of Friends' worship, is a wondrous way to heighten one's individual awareness of God's inner presence. Admittedly such silence may be more fruitful for some persons than for others, yet this very fact is one that should encourage the latter group, for their participation is thus helping others. Reading the testimonies of past members,[22] (which replaces explicit doctrine), is a humbling experience for one like myself, accustomed, for half a century, to being licenced to preach credal belief as being a primary ingredient in seeking one's "salvation".

What believers in God should come to see is that God wants us to work with all others, both those who honestly maintain that God does not exist and also those – doubtless the largest group of all – who see no urgent reason to "decide" on something unprovable either way. I believe that God's priority for us is to affirm in word and action that all persons, including those who are unwilling to acknowledge God's existence, possess the divine nature within. Many who today assert that "there is no God" may never come to realize that there is purpose in every human life, including their own, until those of us who are believers in God commit ourselves to reliance upon our own "ASIA" (Awareness of Shared Interior Authority). In so doing we are able to relinquish what is often perceived by others to be a "carrot-promise": that "reward of eternal life", in favour of replacing it with simple trust in God's loving care.

So many books have been recently written emphasizing the inclusiveness aspect to the "bringing in of God's kingdom" that there is no need for me to attempt to set out here their insights, nor could I do it nearly as well as they have done. It is only a feeling, which has grown from my contact with the Scriptures and the sacraments of the Church over my lifetime, that has induced me to set out this "alternative view": a feeling that it might in some way add weight to such insights of others, and so encourage all persons living today, and tomorrow, to realize that using their special gifts for the healing and reconciling of others is "all to the good".

Here, then, are the eight "Foundations of a true social order" as set forth by the Quakers, prefaced as follows:

They were not intended as rules of life but as an attempt to set forth ideals that are aspects of eternal Truth and the direct outcome of our testimony to the individual worth of the human soul. Though they proclaimed the ending of "restrictions" of sex, they spoke of God as Father and human beings as men and brothers, as was conventional in their time.

1. The Fatherhood of God, as revealed by Jesus Christ, should lead us toward a brotherhood which knows no restriction of race, sex or social class.

2. This brotherhood should express itself in a social order which is directed, beyond all material ends, to the growth of personality truly related to God and man.

3. The opportunity of full development, physical, moral and spiritual, should be assured to every member of the community, man, woman and child. The development of man's full personality should not be hampered by unjust conditions nor crushed by economic pressure.

4. We should seek a way of living that will free us from the bondage of material things and mere conventions, that will raise no barrier between man and man, and will put no excessive burden of labour upon any by reason of our superfluous demands.

5. The spiritual force of righteousness, loving-kindness and trust is mighty because of the appeal it makes to the best in every man, and when applied to industrial relations achieves great things.

6. Our rejection of the methods of outward domination, and of the appeal to force, applies not only to international affairs, but to the whole problem of industrial control. Not through antagonism but through co-operation and goodwill can the best be obtained for each and all.

7. Mutual service should be the principle upon which life is organised. Service, not private gain, should be the motive of all work.

8. The ownership of material things, such as land and capital, should be so regulated as best to minister to the need and development of man.[23]

Although the above statement was set out more than eighty years ago, its message is timeless. Recognizing that it was written in a Christian context, I believe that one might now be permitted to widen the subject of the first Foundation to include manifestations of a loving God revealed both to those who lived in ancient times in parts of the world unknown to those whose story is in our bible, and also to persons today who recognize a spirit of compassion within each member of the human family, right from birth.

Indeed, I believe that one can read from the early gospels that the importance of Jesus' baptism by John was not that the Spirit of God entered him at that point, but that suddenly he had become aware that this Spirit was within him. I regard the analogy ("like a dove") as a dramatic, later, addition in the telling. It is notable that Jesus made no effort to baptize any of his followers nor anyone with whom he came in contact – he gradually came to see that the same Spirit was already within them.

The message is not that Jesus "cleared the way for us", but that he "made the way clear for us", as clear as it is possible for the meaning of one person's life to be comprehended by others. We are to work in harmony with those who do not share our belief in God yet who are willing to work with us for two good reasons: first, that they share in our desire to bring in a better world and second, that they become aware that more and more "believers in God" now claim "eternal life" neither to be "certain" nor "more important" than their work together in this mortal life. It may or may not happen that anyone's "intellectual belief" position will alter, through observation of others' lives. This must be accepted quietly. As our own death approaches, whatever has been our position, the demeanor of those we know around us who believe at least in the possibility of eternal life may affect our own belief. Then, if we were also so to die, trusting, as Jesus did, that to be always in our Father's loving care was completely sufficient, who knows how significantly that might affect those who follow us?

The "humaneness of humanity" has a long way to go: this we all know from its very brief time-span to date, whether visualized as "five minutes in an entire day" or as "a thousand years are but as one day". But God is infinitely patient. May each of us resolve to do our best to set the Spirit free within us, to guide and strengthen our innate desire to do what is right. Thus will humanity's goal of compassion for all eventually be reached.

Notes - Chapter 10 – Freeing the Spirit

1. ODCC 1997, p. 597, Fall, the; pp. 1195-6, Original Sin.

2. Nolan 1992, p. 148.

3. Nolan 1992, pp. 148-149.

4. Nolan 1992, p. 149.

5. Nolan 1992, p. 150.

6. Nolan 1992, p. 150.

7. Nolan 1992, p. 151.

8. Borg & Wright 2000, p. 68.

9. (The Death of Jesus) Mt 27:46-50; Mk 15:34-37.

10. J. Wijngaards, *God Within Us* (Fount, London, 1988), pp. 45-46. This is part of a quotation from Ruysbroeck, which is continued five paragraphs below, see note 13 below.

11. Borg 1998, p. 12.

12. Nolan 1992, p. 151.

13. Wijngaards 1988, pp. 46, 178. He offers his "own free translation of the original Flemish" of J. van Ruysbroeck, *De Gheestelike Brulocht* ("The Spiritual Wedding"), Kompas, Mechelen 1932,Vol. 1, p. 148.

14. (Compassion Towards All) Lk 6:36.

15. Borg & Wright 2000, p. 70.

16. Thomas A. Harris, *I'm OK, You're OK* (Avon Books, New York, 1973).

17. Quakers 1999, Chap. 2.12 [No page numbering after the Introduction]. (For the complete reference for this book, see Bibliography).

18. D. Cupitt, *Taking Leave of God* (SCM Press, London, 1980), pp. 166-7. Professor Cupitt has written a number of books subsequently, I believe largely on this theme.

19. Jesus' summation of "The Law and The Prophets", set out in The Great Commandment (Mt 22:34-40; Mk 12:28-34; Lk 10:25-28), and as elucidated by the parable of The Good Samaritan (Lk 10:29-37).

20. (God needs no 'things' to be sacrificed; an early perception) Ps. 50:10.

21. Quakers 1999, Chap. 21.72.

22. Quakers 1999, Chaps. 27, 28, 29 contain many spiritual insights.

23. Quakers 1999, Chap. 23.16.

Epilogue
The Peril of Paradise-Promising Religions

This epilogue is meant not only for the Christian religion. In this third millennium there are many others, one in particular with the avowed intention of achieving world domination, and seeming to identify religious and political aims. We are told that the terrible events of 11 September 2001 were set in train through the

Note: Although my book was largely complete in its structure by the year 2000, the grotesque catastrophe of 11 September 2001 was terrifying and valid evidence that my message had become both more important and more urgent than before. Therefore I added this Epilogue in 2002.

actions of human beings who sincerely believed that killing a certain kind of other persons, completely defenceless, was "doing God's Will". We have seen the initial response to be primarily one of vengeance, covered politically and morally by the phrase "A War Against Terrorism". The fanatical extremists of the religion of Islam carried out those merciless events; they perceive that God's supreme attribute is *Omnipotence* and that therefore believers must use *power* – at all levels: covert and overt, supernatural and human – to implement the rule of God over the entire world. Those who died carrying out that cowardly attack are exalted by radical Muslims as "The Magnificent 19", now in Paradise.[1]

For Christians, and indeed most of us, the supreme attribute of God is *Love* – respect and concern for others – which is to be practiced in all human relationships. On this basis, a response of "Vengeance with Power" is wrong. Yet through literal readings of Scripture and the "Ark of Salvation" concept, many Christians still believe that they can "climb on board" and escape, through obedient membership in a religious group, a "Flood" of nothingness at death, by "keeping the Faith", which includes the promise of eternal life with God, i.e. Paradise.

Even though both Islamic and Christian theologians may qualify such simple beliefs, it is their common perception that is the difficulty. It does seem to most of us that here are two religions each claiming unique proclamation of both truth and eternal salvation. I believe that both Christianity and Islam must renounce their exclusive claims to "know the truth". Both Jesus and Mohammed may well be seen as inspired prophets, but it is fallible men who have written their biographies and claimed to interpret the meaning of their lives. Each religion claims to be "a religion of the Book", but they are "singing from different Books." And so it has fallen to a leader of an earlier "religion of the Book" – one which was later included in both the others – to see the answer: "God has spoken to mankind in many languages... no one creed has a monopoly on religious truth. In heaven there is truth, on earth there are truths. *God is greater than religion.* He is only partially comprehended by any faith."[2] Accordingly, it is essential that all religions come to realize that non-violence and reconciliation are humanity's only valid keys to peace, and that such peace will be the fulfilment of human destiny.

The continued existence of both the power-structure and membership-importance of competing religious institutions makes it impossible for humanity to achieve its goal of compassion for all people. Study of Jesus' ministry is gradually opening up to reveal that this concept of respect and concern for others, regardless of their statements of belief or non-belief, is imbedded in the human race as a whole. But so much remains to be done before the reality of this "Good Spirit Within" is recognized by those who are taught that it is right to use the animal instinct of force, of dominating others, to do "God's will".

I hope therefore that a book similar in theme to mine will be written about Islam, although probably any person who attempts this will suffer great persecution from their religious authorities. As for Judaism, the necessity for exclusive territorial possession to validate God's favour will surely, if gradually, be seen to be an obsolete idea. One day humanity will recognize that the concept of "sacred places" (for any "religion") is as obsolete as that of "sacred ceremonies", with Jerusalem, Mecca, Rome, and all places linked to religious institutions being set free from the taint of exclusiveness.

As for reviving our own Spirit, I suggest we note how the lives of individuals are now being remembered in more personal fashion. Instead of ritual-driven funerals, where the officiant has often seen fit to overlay the humble virtues of the departed with an ecclesiastical gloss, our society is moving towards memorial services filled with tributes from persons who have shared good relationships with the deceased through the years. Obituaries, too, are inspiring for all who read them – today's writers setting down achievements large or small – the better to encourage recognition of the reality of the Spirit working within us and so sharing in our decisions for action.

Books also can strengthen our wills to join with our inner Spirit. You will find, on the final page of this book, a very brief list. May I commend two of them in particular: The 1999 edition of *Quaker Faith and Practice* is a treasure-house of the writings of many who have discovered how to conjoin human free-will and the inner reality of the Spirit; and Roger Scruton's "*An Intelligent Person's Guide to Philosophy*", which brought philosophy alive for me, shows how "the love of wisdom", flowing with compassion from persons to persons, can enrich us all because it is expressed through so many and such diverse paths.

How greatly it will please God, I believe we shall come gradually to see, as more and more of the human race "lift their hearts" together in mutual thanksgiving for the presence of both life and that "spirit of good" within. It will be a new kind of Pentecost: a Pentecost of the *Inner Spirit*, with no signs of flames of fire coming down from heaven to alight upon certain people,[3] but with all hands raised in gratitude for the inner warmth of knowing that one is alive and that there is a good purpose in each one's life *today*! And so I hope that this third millennium will come to be known as *The Age of the Good Spirit*.

Such are the ways of the recognized and always-reviving spirit within us all.

Notes - Epilogue

1. *The Times* (London, England, 25 August, 2003), p.2, photo of poster which shows nineteen individuals in separate photos around the words "**The Magnificent 19** (in large and bold lettering) That divided the world on September 11th" followed by what I assume to be a quotation from the Koran "... they were youth who believed in their Lord and We increased them in guidance". In the accompanying article headed "Extremist poster celebrates 9/11 killers", one extremist group is quoted as saying that "it intended to place the poster in British cities to advertise a meeting they wanted to hold on the anniversary of the attacks". The group "campaigns for a worldwide Islamic government"; I saw no report of the meeting having been held.

2. Jonathan Sacks, as quoted by Ruth Gledhill, Religion Correspondent, in her article "Chief Rabbi revises his use of word 'truth'", *The Times*, October 25, 2002. (italics mine).

3. (The "Limited" Pentecost) Acts 2:3.

Recognizing The Spirit Within Us

Bibliography

Borg 1995	Borg, M. J., *Meeting Jesus Again For the First Time: The Historical Jesus & The Heart of Contemporary Faith* (HarperSanFrancisco 1995)
Borg 1998	Borg, M. J., *The God We Never Knew: Beyond Dogmatic Religion to a More Authentic Contemporary Faith* (HarperSanFrancisco 1998)
Borg & Wright 2000	Borg, M. J. & Wright, N. T., *The Meaning of Jesus: Two Visions* (HarperSan Francisco 2000)
Brown 1997	Brown, R. E., *An Introduction to the New Testament* (Doubleday New York 1997)
Chilton 2002	Chilton, Bruce, *Rabbi Jesus: An Intimate Biography* (Doubleday New York 2002)
ODCC 1997	Cross, F. L. & Livingstone, E. A., eds *The Oxford Dictionary of the Christian Church* (3rd ed.) (Oxford 1997)
Cupitt 1980	Cupitt, D., *Taking Leave of God* (SCM Press London 1980)
Freeman 2002	Freeman, Charles, *The Closing of the Western Mind* (William Heinemann London 2002)
Hick 1977	Hick, J., ed., *The Myth of God Incarnate* (SCM Press London 1977)
Nolan 1992	Nolan, A., *Jesus Before Christianity* (1976, rev. 1992; Orbis Books Maryknoll New York 1992)
Throckmorton 1992	Throckmorton, B. H., *Gospel Parallels: A Comparison of the Synoptic Gospels* (Thos. Nelson Nashville 1992)
Wijngaards 1988	Wijngaards, J., *God Within Us* (Collins/Fount London 1988)

Quakers 1999   *Quaker faith and practice: The book of Christian discipline of the Yearly Meeting of the Religious Society of Friends (Quakers) in Britain* (2nd ed. rev.) (London 1995-9)

Note: Biblical quotations are taken from the *Holy Bible: New International Version* (New York International Bible Society, 1984).

OTHER WORKS CONSULTED

Cupitt, D., *The Sea of Faith* (BBC 1984)

Forstater, M., *The Spiritual Teachings of Marcus Aurelius* (Hodder & Stoughton, 2000)

Gollancz, V., *A Year of Grace* (1950; Penguin Books 1955)

Grant, S., *Towards An Alternative Theology* (ATC Bangalore 1991)

Hesse, H., *Siddhartha* (1922; Pan Books/Picador edn. 1991)

Scruton, R., *An Intelligent Person's Guide to Philosophy* (Duckworth 1996)

Printed in the United States
by Baker & Taylor Publisher Services